Mallard

Don   : became nationally famous for his tireless – and ultimately
succ   l – campaign, while editor of the *Matlock Mercury* newspaper,
to c   he name of Stephen Downing, imprisoned for 27 years for
the   ler of a Derbyshire woman. It won him the OBE and was
ack   edged to have righted a major miscarriage of justice. He
sub   atly told the story of his campaign in his best-selling book
Tow   out Pity, and has since been involved in several other
succe   campaigns. Formerly a professional footballer for Bury
and B   burn, and a journalist for the *Manchester Evening News*,
he liv.   North Wales.

MALLARD

How the 'Blue Streak' Broke the
World Speed Record

D O N   H A L E

First published in Great Britain
2005 by Aurum Press Ltd
7 Greenland Street, London NW1 0ND

This paperback edition first published in 2008.

ISBN 978 1 84513 345 0

1 3 5 7 9 8 6 4 2
2009 2011 2012 2010 2008

Edited by Andrew Roden

This book is dedicated to the memory of Sir Nigel Gresley,
one of the country's most brilliant railway engineers –
and a national hero

Contents

	Preface	ix
1	The Races to the North	1
2	Nigel Gresley and the Great Northern	11
3	The London and North Eastern Railway	23
4	The *Flying Scotsman*	39
5	Developments across the Channel	51
6	Streamlined Efficiency	62
7	Faster and Faster	76
8	The Germans Increase the Pressure	99
9	The LMS Draws Ahead	112
10	*Mallard* Spreads Her Wings	123
11	The Day of Reckoning	136
12	After the Record	155
	Acknowledgements	167
	Bibliography	169
	Index	171

Preface

Imagine, if you will, travelling back in time to witness the final flickering of a golden age. You wouldn't need to go as far as you think, in years or in distance. Say 1960, or perhaps a year or so later; the location, the largely flat countryside of west Lincolnshire a few miles south of Grantham.

It was a time when summers were endless and blazing hot. In the evening, when the heat of the day starts to ebb away, imagine taking a walk through fields of ripening wheat to a nearby railway cutting. Picture leaning against a fence for a while, just relaxing, enjoying the wonderful scene. But for boys of all ages, as a book once said, this place is far more significant than a mere beauty spot: it is a place where history was made.

A procession of modern diesel trains rumbles past – their locomotives are heavy, cumbersome and no more powerful than the steam locomotives they are rapidly replacing. They may be one of the wonders of the age, but aesthetically they are just 'boxes on wheels', all the wonder of what makes them work hidden inside.

Then, the wind carries the faint trace of a siren – it could be mistaken for the wail of an air raid, but those haven't sounded for fifteen years. No, this is something much more exciting than an air raid. Minutes later, the faint sounds of a steam engine make their presence known. Still some miles away, it's working hard and approaching fast. There's no towering column of smoke, meaning whatever is coming is really moving, and then it's there. With the clatter of the coaches beating a tattoo on the rails, the engine rounds the bend and attacks the hill. But this is no ordinary engine – the shape gives the game away. She's no longer in pristine condition and streaks of grime are visible on her smooth aerodynamic casing. But, like a fading actress, she still has her admirers and can still give a winning performance. She was built for speed, and even at 70mph lopes gracefully, seemingly secure in the knowledge she could go much faster if she really wanted to. The engine may be going fast, but it's almost silent, the loudest noise that of wheel on track and of the coaches behind. As she gets almost level, the driver blows the whistle again. Another wailing scream that starts in defiance but gradually fades into a low moan of resigned acceptance, and with a clatter of carriages rattling away behind, she's gone, racing on the way north.

If this is not quite the final curtain of a golden age, it's certainly close to the last act of an era that saw breathtaking courage, sublime skill and artistry of the highest order produce one of the finest feats of engineering ever: a superbly streamlined, exquisite masterpiece of a steam locomotive called *Mallard*.

My own interest in railways began more than forty years ago, during a now-forgotten era, when my brother and I would travel the country as rail enthusiasts or train spotters. Nowadays, we would be called 'anoraks' and probably banished to the far end of some dilapidated platform at a mainline terminus. I had little interest in diesels or electric trains then, simply preferring the power and majesty of steam. The A4 Pacific class are still my personal favourites – to see an A4 flat-out in full cry was certainly a sight to behold: they hurtled through the Scottish Lowlands during family holidays and, if I close my eyes, I can still hear their shrill whistles. It's the kind of scene I remember vividly more than four decades on, and that inspired me to write this book.

Don Hale
March 2005

Chapter One
The Races to the North

Mention the term 'arms race' and one instinctively thinks in terms of military build-ups in the twentieth century: the Dreadnoughts of 1904–14, the Spitfires and Messerschmitt 109s of the 1930s, and the space race of the 1960s. All were politically motivated, and all had consequences that would change the way we live. But arms races aren't always about weapons. In the 1930s, an equally exciting competition between Britain and Germany was taking place on the railways. Throughout that decade, records would be made and broken, culminating in a high-speed run in 1938 by the famous locomotive *Mallard* that has never been bettered since by steam traction.

It was a hugely significant event that went beyond the breaking of a speed record: at a point when Nazi Germany seemed to be having everything its own way, Britain's triumph proved that ingenuity and determination could beat the Nazi regime. At a time when British morale was faltering, this success provided a much-needed fillip. *Mallard* is significant in other ways, too: her creation marked the culmination of more than a hundred years of steady development for the steam locomotive, and her record-breaking sprint from Grantham to Peterborough set the high-water mark for railways everywhere. Despite all the technological breakthroughs that have happened since, *Mallard* still represents for many the zenith of the railway's golden age, before war followed by nationalisation and then re-privatisation saw its painful decline. How *Mallard*'s triumph was achieved, and why, forms the subject of this book.

The desire to go faster, higher, farther seems to be an intrinsic part of human nature, which is why, in 1804, a Cornish engineer called Richard Trevithick invented the steam locomotive. The desire to make money is another intrinsic desire, which is also why colliery owners in north-east England started to use steam locomotives, as they could haul more than horses.

At the famous Rainhill Trials in 1829, Robert Stephenson's *Rocket* reached a frightening 29mph, and less than twenty years later the unprecedented speed of 60mph was the norm on some railways. These were the fastest machines ever invented at that time – the equivalent of a rocket today – and any speed advantage was immediately seized on by the companies involved to promote their routes and win new business.

For the railways, going faster was a deadly serious competition, with the various railway works around the country pushing materials and manufacturing techniques to their limit. At first, the Great Western Railway, with its flat route from London to Bristol and wider tracks than anyone else, held the advantage. By the 1860s, however, other companies had caught up. These were heady times, but because each company operated on generally different routes, it was difficult to compare performances on a like-for-like basis. This didn't deter two alliances from competing with each other in a series of races that lasted years (with occasional interruptions) and effectively set the pattern for the story of *Mallard*.

The rivalry lay between the two routes to Scotland – the West Coast Main Line from London Euston through Rugby, Stafford, Preston and Carlisle, and the East Coast route, which ran from London King's Cross through Peterborough, Doncaster, York, Darlington and Newcastle to Edinburgh; both still run today. The first railway route from London to Glasgow and Edinburgh, up the West Coast of England, was completed in 1847 and operated jointly by the London & North Western Railway Company and the Caledonian Railway Company. The rival line, the slightly shorter East Coast route, opened some four years later following an alliance between the Great Northern, North Eastern and

North British railway companies. 'Speed' soon became the buzz-word of the period. Within ten years of opening the East Coast line, its operators were proudly boasting that they offered a much faster schedule than their rivals. Unlike today's heated competition between budget airlines, in which the key factor is who offers the lowest fares, price was no issue: speed was all.

At this time the railway operators had a rather unfortunate image. They were the butt of newspaper jokes and often mocked by caricaturists of the day. The public expected that trains would be cold, dirty, smelly, slow and downright uncomfortable – and they were usually right. Imagine ten or more hours in a third class compartment, with oil lighting, no heating and wooden seats, sometimes upholstered but still painful for long periods – not a pleasant experience. But with the only alternative being several days in a horse-drawn carriage, there was little choice for anyone who wanted to go to Scotland, or anywhere else for that matter.

In many ways, the railways reflected social and economic change – paradoxically, change which the railways themselves had engineered. Massive construction challenges and manufacturing problems had been overcome, and the railways provided a means to move produce rapidly. As more lines opened, people began to commute into work. For the railways, gaining the hearts and minds of this expanding clientele was vital.

Backed by their new, 'racing style' image, the directors of many railway companies determined to lose their old-fashioned tag and re-invent themselves. First, they began to encourage fast services from London northwards: to the growing industrial centres of Sheffield, Manchester and Birmingham and, of course, across the borders to Scotland. However, at this early stage, they also promoted quality and convenience rather than pure speed.

Then, between 1872 and 1876, the Midland Railway Company decided to build its own line from Settle to Carlisle, which enabled it to bypass the existing LNWR route from Crewe to Carlisle and thus set up its own service to Scotland. Even more importantly, it confirmed plans to admit third class passengers to all of its services for the first time in its history. The news came as a bombshell to many of the other class-ridden railway operators, especially to the rather highbrow East and West Coast firms. Then, a few weeks later, they received a second shock: the Midland Railway said it was also going to scrap the second class service and upgrade third. It could now justifiably boast its trains were more luxurious than the competition.

At this stage, the East Coast service in particular had been content with competing for the quality of its passengers rather than the quantity, but this new series of statements from their Midland rivals meant that they now faced serious competition and risked losing a large part of their market. In response the *Scotsman* service finally admitted third class passengers and announced a new running time of nine hours.

Disturbed by the threat of further competition from a new rival and by the constant and infuriating boasts of 'superior speed and revised schedules' from the East Coast line, in May 1887 the West Coast management team unexpectedly rebelled. They announced that they would not only match their competitors but beat them, with a new operating schedule of just nine hours from London to Edinburgh – exactly the same time as the rival train the 'Scotsman', with a broad hint they could, and probably would, improve on that.

This bold move led to renewed boasts from all sides, which not only attracted interest but also rallied public support. The foreign press soon picked up the story and for many months the directors of several continental railway companies kept a watching brief on developments. Any news, no matter how trivial, was eagerly gobbled up and reported by the volatile and jingoistic British press. In those years the newly united Germany, fresh from its success in the Franco-Prussian war, was building up its military in a bid to acquire an Empire along the same lines as Britain's. National superiority was vital.

By 1 August 1887, less than four months after the West Coast first launched their high-speed programme, the East and West Coast outfits began running head-to-head from London to Scotland – eventually revising an already punishing schedule to just eight hours. At first the two companies seemed fairly well matched, but all this changed when the East Coast Company deliberately tried to take the lead. Determined not to lose out, they vowed to reduce the 'Scotsman''s running time to just 7 hours and 45 minutes, and ran a special test train to prove the point. This recorded an outstanding performance, racing from London to Edinburgh in just 7 hours and 27 minutes, twenty minutes under the advertised schedule – even allowing for a near half-hour stop at York for lunch and an unexpected delay caused by a swing bridge at Selby.

The East Coast management were elated by their success, but realised that it came at a cost. Running trains at such high speeds was becoming increasingly expensive in terms of maintenance, and there were safety issues too; a derailment or, even worse, a crash would be a disaster for all concerned. The day after the record-breaking run, the directors of both alliances met and reluctantly agreed to a compromise, a more conservative schedule of just under 8 hours and 30 minutes. To the great disappointment of the public and doubtless some of the drivers (but perhaps not the hard-pressed firemen) the racing stopped – at least for a few years.

Meanwhile, British engineering continued to expand the frontiers of possibility with the opening of the Tay Bridge in 1887 and the Forth Bridge in 1890. These magnificent structures reduced the East Coast journey from London to Aberdeen to 523.5 miles, against the West Coast distance of 540 miles, and overall journey time to 12 hours and 20 minutes from King's Cross. There were unprecedented demands from the public for new trials; the press continued to focus on the issue and observers from across the world waited eagerly to see what would happen next.

They were not disappointed. In June 1895, determined not to be beaten again, the West Coast alliance entered the fray, recording a new world record time of 11 hours and 45 minutes from Euston to Aberdeen. Its rivals were not slow to respond, and for a thrilling seventeen days in July and August every night became a race to the finish, with timetables continually updated until the drivers of both services were told to cast schedules aside to make the best time they could.

On each of those nights, two express trains left London's King's Cross and Euston stations at 8 p.m., one on each route and both bound for Aberdeen. For the final thirty-eight miles of the journey, from Kinnaber Junction, near Montrose, to Aberdeen, the East Coast train had to use West Coast tracks. Whoever reached Kinnaber Junction first would win the race, as strict intervals were enforced between trains running on the same track. The story goes that on one run, the trains were neck and neck and within sight of each other as they steamed furiously towards Kinnaber Junction. The signalman, who worked for the Caledonian Railway, had to decide which train to let onto the section first. In a sporting gesture, he gave the 'road' to the East Coast train – but it was as close as a race could be. Still, it was a little difficult to decide who had actually won, so the companies agreed to a change of tactics and switched back again to competing over running times instead of head-to-head parallel running.

On 20 August 1895 the East Coast express crew really excelled themselves. The train arrived at Edinburgh Waverley in just 6 hours 19 minutes, then continued onward to Aberdeen in a superb combined time of 8 hours 40 minutes from London. This achievement claimed another world record and the Aberdeen through time remained on the books for eighty years, only beaten by the introduction of 100mph-plus diesel trains travelling the same route. The timings belie the sheer difficulty of running fast with steam locomotives. During the Aberdeen races, vital stops were needed on the East Coast route, and locomotives were changed at Grantham, York and Newcastle to avoid running out of fuel. Despite this, the train still managed to claim another record, achieving an average speed of more than 60mph for the entire journey – including the difficult gradient from Edinburgh to Aberdeen with a 100-ton load.

The next evening, the London & North Western and Caledonian Railway, determined to claim their share of glory, attacked the same target via their own West Coast route. They, too, had to make engine changes, this time at Crewe, Carlisle and Perth, and they also had to negotiate severe climbs at Shap Summit in the Lake District (915ft) and at Beattock (1015ft), with three coaches in a seventy-ton load. Although they did not quite overtake the running time of their rivals, they recorded another magnificent record, achieving a superb time of just 8 hours 42 minutes from London, for a journey that was some seventeen miles longer, and a higher average speed of 63.3mph. These were remarkable achievements that pushed the technology of the day to its limits. They also set in stone the rivalry between East and West Coast routes that still exists to this day.

By the following year, many other national railway operators were also competing hard on speed. It suddenly seemed to be the craze of the nation: fast expresses now departed several times a day from the opposition London stations to Manchester, usually arriving within five minutes of each other. Press statements claimed racing trains rarely stopped for anything – including stations – and staff were instructed to give them priority. Timetables were discarded and drivers adopted a 'gung-ho' spirit, determined to be the first to reach Scotland, at almost any cost. Drivers and train crews certainly needed all their experience on the difficult northern routes, yet some began to take chances, realising that valuable minutes could be won or lost by successfully negotiating major obstacles at crossover points and junctions, or on sharp track curves. Some unscrupulous railway directors even reduced the number of coaches hauled, just to maintain top speed and give their trains a sporting chance. Despite other exciting runs on other cross-country services, it was the Scottish races that remained firmly in the public spotlight. The public remained curious, eager to know every minute detail about the contestants. Press coverage became intense – in one story, it was claimed that the races had encouraged gambling.

Inevitably, other mainline services, including freight, were affected. It was hard to run a reliable freight or local passenger service when the line ahead might be shut down unpredictably to allow the 'Scotsman' through. Locomotives at the time were not equipped with speedometers (which were not standard on all railways until the late 1940s), so the authorities, concerned for public safety, insisted on the installation of track markers and mileage posts at quarter-mile distances. Even so the line between calculated risk and outright danger was increasingly being crossed, especially at major junctions. The issue was of such concern that it was even debated in parliament. Fortunately, there were few mishaps or breakdowns during the speed runs. But in August 1896, a southbound express was derailed at Preston when it exceeded the speed limit entering the station. The two engines came to rest against a bridge wall with the coaches scattered across the tracks. Fortunately there were only sixteen passengers on board, but one was killed.

The races were not an unmixed blessing even for the companies who initiated them. Many trains were double-headed and used numerous locomotives en route to haul coaches at speed. Maintenance costs soared, but despite keen public interest, passenger numbers fell disappointingly. Consequently the directors of both companies agreed that in future they would concentrate on improving their services.

Other railway operators were still interested in breaking

records. The Great Western Railway and London & South Western Railway began to stage their own spectacular competitions. In 1904 the GWR threw down a spectacular gauntlet, with a run from Plymouth to London that still ranks as one of the most daring railway operations ever. On 9 May that year, one of its new City class locomotives, No. 3440, *City of Truro*, became the fastest train on British rails, with a timer on the train recording a top speed of 102.3mph. This figure has been disputed since and never officially recognised, but the balance of evidence suggests that whatever the top speed actually was, it was certainly around the magic hundred-mark.

After this, to the disappointment of many, most companies thought the records could wait. Railway technology was at its limit: to achieve faster speeds locomotives would have to become radically more powerful, with longer range. Even as the West and East Coast railways were busy racing, designers across the world were scratching their heads trying to work out how to provide a new generation of rolling stock to haul the heavy loads now being demanded, and luxurious carriages to attract new business. The emphasis quickly changed from speed to increased capacity and passenger comfort. Engineers concentrated on building more powerful locomotives and new rolling stock to carry heavier loads for greater profits.

The speed trials might be over, but their effects were long lasting. They had not only accelerated journey times but also provided a valuable impetus for the development of new locomotives and rolling stock. The achievements on the London–Scotland routes and elsewhere helped shape the future of the industry, and the investment poured into the railway network by competitive bosses provided skilled training and regular work for employees across the country.

The results also ensured Britain continued to rule the tracks, holding more than a dozen early, fully authenticated steam records. It was many years before overseas nations were able to mount any serious challenge, and in the meantime the British rail industry had not only gained acres of publicity at home but also attracted worldwide attention and admiration. Those eagerly awaiting the next races to the north would have to be patient. It would be another forty years before the successor companies on the two main lines succumbed once again to the allure of speed.

Chapter Two
Nigel Gresley and the Great Northern

A round the time of the 1895 races to the north, Nigel Gresley, a young apprentice with the London & North Western Railway (LNWR), was employed at Crewe, Cheshire. While he must have watched the races with interest, he could not have known that some forty years later he would force the statisticians to rewrite their record books. For an observer of the 1890s, Gresley's creations would have seemed beyond belief.

Born in Edinburgh on 19 June 1876, Gresley was the fourth son of the Reverend Nigel Gresley. He spent his early childhood years at the family home in Netherseale, near Swadlincote in Derbyshire, a comfortable existence with several live-in servants. Although Gresley came from a privileged background, he probably had the railway in his blood from birth: he was almost born on a train when his mother, Joanna, was forced to visit the Scottish capital whilst heavily pregnant. She had travelled to Edinburgh to see a specialist because she was suffering from problems in her pregnancy. It was a brave decision, for the experience would have been extremely slow, uncomfortable and arduous, requiring a journey via Burton on Trent to Derby, and then onward by a precarious schedule and numerous stops and starts to Scotland.

While she was in Scotland, Joanna Gresley gave birth in a lodging house at number 14 Dublin Street, a location probably influenced by the Reverend William Douglas, a close relative who lived at an adjacent property. The child was given the first name Herbert after one of his godfathers, and then Nigel, as a link to family ancestors dating back to Norman times. Perhaps pride in their heredity also partly explains the family's unusually competitive spirit: family members were able to trace their roots back many generations to Robert de Toesni, who accompanied William the Conqueror at the Battle of Hastings in 1066. After the Norman Conquest, the family took their name from the local village of Church Gresley, later making their home in nearby Drakelow in South Derbyshire. Gresley's mother, Joanna Wilson, was a local resident hailing from Barton-under-Needwood.

The infant Gresley accompanied his mother home from Edinburgh by train. His father was the rector at St Peter's church in the village, continuing a long-standing family tradition, and it was understood, if not expected, that young Gresley would follow in his father's footsteps. But from an early age he told friends of his desire to become an engine driver, an unusual ambition for someone of his class in the days before a model railway became an essential possession for a small boy. Given his sheltered lifestyle, it certainly seems odd that he should want to get his hands dirty in some form of industrial occupation. But even as a child Gresley clearly possessed an individual streak that would serve him well in years to come. Perhaps he was influenced by newspaper reports about the great races, or was simply fascinated by watching and listening to shunting operations on the nearby colliery branch line. He certainly seems to have been a railway enthusiast from an early age – and there are many cases where a child living next to a railway has gone on to work in them.

Gresley was sent away from Netherseale to attend preparatory school at Barham House, at St Leonard's in Sussex, before completing his studies at Marlborough College. He enjoyed drawing and mechanical engineering and later won a science prize, distinguishing himself in both chemistry and German. His school reports also mentioned some success as a carpenter and noted that he was 'very creative and good with his hands'. Little is known of his schooldays, but one imagines he had a typically

Victorian education – the type designed to breed serious, solid, able empire-builders.

When Gresley left the college in July 1893 aged seventeen, he chose not to continue in formal education, finally confirming his unwillingness to enter the clergy. His family must have been disappointed, but they didn't prevent him going for his chosen career. A young man of Gresley's undoubted ability had many options, and he opted for a future in mechanical engineering on the railways – a job far removed from that of his father. In October that year, he gained employment as a premium apprentice at the Crewe works of the London & North Western Railway Company, under the watchful eye of Frank Webb, the chief mechanical engineer, and works manager Henry Earl.

When Nigel Gresley first started work he was paid the grand sum of four shillings per week but by the time he had completed his apprenticeship he was drawing a respectable wage of twenty-four shillings. The LNWR's Crewe works was a fascinating place then, one of the biggest factories in the country, and one on which the Cheshire town depended. Renowned worldwide, it was as good a place as any for a young man to learn about railway engineering. However, despite the excellence of the factory, the works were frequently called upon to produce a series of bizarre and often poor locomotives. It was a good chance for an aspiring engineer to see what worked, and, just as importantly, what did not. Part of Gresley's studies coincided with the miners' strike of 1893–4 and he was able to gauge at first hand the reaction of many working-class railway workers as severe job losses, and then the restrictions of a four-day working week, began to hit home.

Following his apprenticeship, Gresley spent time in the fitting and erecting shops at Crewe works, where he gained further practical experience. He then moved to the drawing office of the Lancashire & Yorkshire Railway at Horwich, Lancashire, where some very advanced locomotives were being designed. There he studied as a pupil again under John Aspinall, the chief mechanical engineer. At Horwich, Gresley worked in the test room and gained additional experience in the materials laboratory before moving to Blackpool as running-shed foreman. After less than a decade, this young man was starting to move up the career ladder.

In 1901, Gresley met and married Ethel Fullager, the daughter of a solicitor, from Lytham St Annes. She was two years older than her husband and an accomplished musician who had spent time in Germany studying the piano and violin. In the next few years two sons and two daughters were born to the couple, and Gresley became a devoted father, enjoying going on holiday with his children and taking them round the GNR locomotive yards to show them how the great engines were put together.

Through rapid promotion, Gresley then moved to become an outdoor assistant in the carriage and wagon department, transferring to Newton Heath, near Manchester. In 1902 he was made the works manager and then, after a reshuffle, was appointed assistant to the works superintendent. He was one of the youngest people in that kind of position on the railway, and already it was becoming clear that he was set for high office. Just over a year later, Gresley successfully applied for the position of superintendent with the carriage and wagon department on the Great Northern Railway. It was a big leap for him, in terms of both location and the opportunities it offered. He quickly made his mark, however, radically changing the shape of coaches from the fussy clerestory roof (which had a raised strip running down the middle to let light in) to a neater elliptical roof, which made the coaches seem much more airy. Thanks to Gresley's efforts at chassis design, the vehicles rode better, and he even found the time to upgrade the comfort of the interiors. The position carried a salary of £750 a year and seemed a good career move but in March 1905, still in his twenties, he moved again.

This time he went to a senior posting at Doncaster works, as subordinate to the well known and highly respected chief mechanical engineer, Henry Ivatt. The move advanced still further Gresley's rapid rise up the promotional ladder and provided him with an ideal base from which to learn, watch and wait. It was a highly prestigious position for someone so young: at precisely the right time, he had succeeded in putting his name into lights within a very large shop window. Even Gresley, though, cannot have known how much bigger that shop window would become in less than twenty years.

Of his personal life at this stage, rather less is known. Like many in his position at the time, Gresley seems to have been shy of publicity, leaving us with few indications of what he was really like. What we can say with certainty is that he was a keen sportsman who enjoyed tennis, golf, shooting and occasional rock climbing. He was also a mountain of a man, powerfully built, and with seemingly boundless enthusiasm. He towered above his friends and colleagues, who fondly called him 'Tim', a comical abbreviation of 'Tiny Tim'. Several employees called him 'Mr G' or the 'Great White Chief', and later, following his knighthood, 'Sir Nigel'.

This all suggests quite a likeable man, but Gresley was not popular with everyone. He was shrewd and ambitious and some claimed he was an opportunist – he was certainly a master of diplomacy, and a man who knew exactly what he wanted and just how to get it. These skills would prove crucial in his rise to the top: pure ability is rarely enough to survive the guerrilla warfare and politics that accompany life in every big company. Henry Ivatt once claimed Gresley was 'too pushy and too self-confident'. Others claimed he was 'downright difficult' to work with; the GNR board, however, welcomed his enthusiasm, honesty and obvious prudence with finance. He was rather old-fashioned and expected staff to speak only when they were spoken to. Yet he seems to have retained a dry sense of humour and loved entertaining friends on golfing breaks.

In January 1910, Gresley's promising career and active social calendar almost came to a premature end when he received a horrific injury that nearly cost him his leg and very nearly his life. The accident happened while visiting his mother at Turnditch in Derbyshire. He was out shooting rooks with his brother and, as he climbed a large hedge, a blackthorn spike wedged deeply into his leg. The thorn was extremely difficult to extract and his brother could only remove it with the aid of a penknife, which was normally used to clean his pipe. The wound became infected and both phlebitis and septicaemia set in.

Gresley was desperately ill for many weeks and his doctor thought his leg might have to be amputated. The chairman of the Great Northern Railway, Lord Allerton, organised for Gresley to be seen by a London specialist, who agreed with the doctor. The specialist made two journeys north, intent on amputation, before agreeing to try to cleanse the wound by using leeches. Fortunately, the treatment worked and the wound healed, and Gresley was able to return home after a brief period of convalescence in Bournemouth. His leg remained tender for some time, and he had a special felt cushion fitted to the underside of his desk to try to prevent undue pressure. Within a short time, though, he was able to return to normal, and eventually travelled north to once again enjoy his outdoor pastimes in the Scottish Highlands.

When Ivatt retired in September 1911, Gresley, aged just thirty-five, was appointed in his place. This was remarkably young for such a demanding role – the equivalent of a general in the army, who would never have promoted so relatively inexperienced a man to the position. Nor was it common practice in other areas of business. It was a calculated gamble by the GNR board. With the title of chief mechanical engineer of the Great Northern Railway, Gresley began his duties in October. His position included control of locomotive running in addition to a host of other responsibilities involving rolling stock, fixtures and fittings.

To the observer, fast passenger locomotives are incomparably the most glamorous and exciting animals in the railway jungle. They're typically big, with a high-set boiler that makes them look bigger still. The wheels are large – up to 6ft 8in – which means when they move they have that wonderful appearance of galloping like a racehorse. And of course, they're fast. When one passes at 70mph or so, you experience a marvellous barrage of sensations – first the sound of the beast snorting its way towards you, then the rushing clatter of wheels and steam as it speeds past, followed by the urgent clickety-clack of the coaches as it heads away. For sheer spectacle, then as now, there is little to beat the sight of an express steam train working hard and fast.

It is surprising to learn then that, of all types of trains, express passenger locomotives were often the least significant. Up until the 1960s, the vast majority of the railway's income came from freight. Back then, if you wanted something moving, it had to go by rail. From racing pigeons to grain to huge girders for industry, everything was loaded onto freight trains at one of the many thousands of freight terminals around the country. When Gresley started work the GNR was desperately short of freight engines and Gresley naturally concentrated his efforts there. The existing passenger locomotives were up to the task – though demands in both loads and speed were increasing and obviously something more powerful would soon be needed.

Like other chief mechanical engineers settling into such an enormous job, at first Gresley perpetuated the designs of his predecessors. Many of the existing locomotives were reasonably adequate but others were limited by a sheer lack of speed. New stock was needed immediately and designing from scratch would take some time. Gresley, as innovative as he undoubtedly was, also had a strongly pragmatic streak. The old designs might not be as good as those he could come up with, but they were available more or less off the shelf, and would have to do until he came up with something better.

At the time, the typical freight locomotive used across the country had six wheels under the boiler, all coupled together to increase grip on the rails. This made them an o-6-o in the standard notation used then and now. The first figure gives the number of guiding wheels, at the front of the locomotive, which guide it around curves. The second is the number of wheels linked to the pistons, the driving wheels, which are coupled by rods and provide the moving force. The final figure is the number of wheels behind the driving wheels; frequently, as in this case, there were none, but on bigger locomotives such wheels were often necessary to provide support for the cab and firebox, and supply additional guidance around bends. These o-6-o freight engines were typically rather small, and had small wheels, which increased grip further because more could be fitted in a given space – six wheels, say, against four of a much larger diameter. But these small wheels limited the locomotive's speed, length and power; if its size was increased without adding more wheels, pronounced overhangs at the front and rear of the locomotive would have made it horribly unstable.

All this was known at the time, and in the early 1910s the GNR's rival Great Western Railway had made a major leap forward by placing a pair of guiding wheels at the front of an o-6-o chassis, turning it into a 2-6-o, or mogul as the arrangement is known. The GWR was far from the first to try this, but what it managed successfully was to make a workable design for freight trains capable of hauling express passenger trains if necessary. The wheel arrangement allowed GWR to lengthen the design significantly, and that meant it could use larger wheels, allowing the locomotive to work less hard at high speeds. The diameter chosen was 5ft 7in – a good compromise between the 4ft 7in wheels used on heavy freight engines, and the 6ft 8in wheels used on express passenger designs.

Ever mindful of developments elsewhere, however, Gresley looked closely at the GWR design and performance and instantly recognised this or something like it as the solution to his own needs. Gresley's first design, a 2-6-0 locomotive produced to haul passenger and goods trains, appeared in 1912, and was called the K1. It was just what the GNR needed, and follow-on orders proved highly successful. Gresley then turned his attention to the challenge of hauling heavy freight trains, and designed a 2-8-0 type, which offered better grip than the moguls, but at the expense of lower speed. He followed this up with a development of his 2-6-0 with a larger boiler, giving more power. These were called K2s. So far so conventional, even by the standards of other railways.

Gresley started preparing new express designs ready for building around 1914, but with the shooting of Archduke Ferdinand in 1914 and the start of the First World War, almost all railway innovation was subordinated until the end of hostilities four years later. Gresley remained at the railway from 1914 to 1918, throughout the war, while Doncaster works was hastily forced to switch to the manufacture of armaments. Gresley later received a CBE for his supervisory work at the plant during this difficult period.

Owing to the immediate post-war recession and later technical problems, it was 1922 before the Doncaster plant returned primarily to locomotive production. For Gresley, this delay proved to be a good thing: it gave him time to appraise his designs carefully without the pressure of needing to build them soon. In doing so, he soon found the answer to one of the Great Northern's pressing needs: a locomotive that could haul heavier and faster freight trains, as well as taking on passenger work effectively if needed.

This was the 2-8-0 with three cylinders, which he built in 1918, paving the way for much more powerful locomotives. It was a radical departure for the Great Northern Railway, and for British practice as a whole. The secret of the new model lay in the number of cylinders that the steam was fed to. Traditionally, almost all locomotives in Britain had two cylinders, either between the wheels or outside them with one on each side. This simple design was adequate for most tasks, but could damage the track because the force of the moving metal was always either on one side or the other, giving a pronounced to-and-fro motion, and a left-to-right one as well. It also limited the amount of power an engine could use: at a certain point, in order to use all the steam a big boiler will generate, the cylinders have to be bigger. Between the wheels, there is something like four feet of useable space, and outside, less than two feet either side. This poses a challenge for the designer seeking to build a really big locomotive – how do you create enough cylinder space to use all the steam? The answer, for most designers in Britain, was to have a cylinder on each side, and two between the wheels, giving a four-cylinder locomotive. The Great Western – which until the First World War was the most innovative railway in the country – had investigated four-cylinder locomotives and was using them very successfully, and this was initially what Gresley had in mind.

But the Great Northern's inventive new CME thought he could create something even better by using three, larger cylinders, with just one between the wheels. This would provide an even start, with the pistons at three different but balanced positions, and would lessen stress on the track caused by reciprocating masses. Even on four-cylinder engines, the balancing was never going to be as good. So it was, then, that the 2-8-0 became the first of a long-lived family of three-cylindered locomotives.

Gresley's innovation didn't stop simply with the number of cylinders. One of the hardest, most awkward and dangerous tasks on the railway was that of oiling the many joints in the rods that linked the cylinders to the driving axle. On almost all locomotives in the country, these rods – the valve gear – were placed between the wheels in order to hide them. The Victorian habit of covering up unsightly things was still going strong, but Gresley decided to break with tradition. He took what was then the unusual step of placing the valve gear outside the wheels where it could be easily and safely maintained. This would have been good for a two-cylinder locomotive, but in his three-cylinder design, the maintenance staff would still have had to go between the wheels to check the gear. Gresley's masterstroke was to link the right and left cylinders in such a way that as their valves opened and closed, they worked the middle valve gear, dramatically easing the servicing of locomotives and at the same time cutting construction costs. His design was always controversial because it needed regular attention at engine sheds to ensure it continued to work. However, Gresley knew it made possible the smooth drive and power output his designs would need.

The 2-8-0 proved a success, and after further tests and studies Gresley introduced his third design of 2-6-0, the K3. These had massive six-foot-diameter boilers, among the widest in Britain at the time of their introduction in 1920. Free-running and powerful, they proved adept at a wide range of work, though they sometimes rode roughly, giving the driver and fireman a good shaking.

With the K3s in traffic and proving broadly successful, Gresley turned his mind to the thorny problem of providing a new generation of express passenger locomotives for the Great Northern Railway. The obvious move was to expand the highly successful 4-4-2 Ivatt designs (called Atlantics for their wheel arrangement, which originated on the east coast of America) into a 4-6-2 (known as Pacifics because they are bigger than Atlantics). This would have increased capacity by 50 per cent, allowing for a much bigger and more powerful design. With this in mind, Gresley took one of the Ivatt engines, No. 3279, which had two cylinders, and rebuilt it with four. J.H. Harrison, a former premium apprentice under Gresley, reckons the locomotive was not a success and certainly Gresley himself never considered four-cylinder expansion for the rest of his career. He scrapped his original proposal for a Pacific design.

Gresley was convinced that a three-cylinder layout would be ideal and undertook extensive research to see if anyone had made such a radical departure from convention succeed elsewhere: somebody had. The Pennsylvania Railroad in the USA had faced similar problems to Gresley, and, after exhaustive studies, produced one of the classic designs of all time – the K4 class Pacific. It was fast, powerful and free steaming, exactly what the Great Northern needed. There was only one problem: it was far too big to run on British railways. Gresley was impressed and decided to draw inspiration from its outstanding features. The wide firebox allowed more coal to be burnt, increasing the heating capacity of the boiler. The combustion chamber, a high-level forward extension of the furnace, allowed the gases of burning coal to be burned more thoroughly, and the conjugated valve gear? Well, Gresley had something similar in mind for his K3s.

In fact, what Gresley ended up with for his first express passenger design was remarkably like a K4 scaled down to fit Britain, and cleaned up somewhat. The design team set to work on a revolutionary new breed of 'super locomotive' that would transform expectations of what the railways could deliver. The stage was set for the construction of the first of the A1 class.

Pacific No. 1470 *Great Northern* appeared from Doncaster works in April 1922, to the shock of enthusiastic press and general observers alike. She was, simply, a giant, eclipsing everything else on the rails in Britain with the exception of a solitary Great Western Pacific. With her gigantic boiler, she clearly had the capacity to steam at high power for long periods, but she was also graceful. It's no coincidence that so many of her progeny would be named after racehorses, because that's what *Great Northern* was: many tonnes of thoroughbred iron racing horse. Gresley's genius had been thrust into the public spotlight for the first time.

Chapter Three
The London and North Eastern Railway

While Gresley was revolutionising locomotive design, the rail industry itself was undergoing significant changes. At the beginning of the First World War, the 123 miscellaneous railway companies that once criss-crossed the nation were temporarily 'nationalised' to form a united operation to support the war effort. This central control of the railway system worked, confirming the long-held belief that the railways were that rare and (in those non-socialist times) not wholly desirable thing, a natural monopoly. The railways performed prodigious feats, moving everything from troops to tanks around the country.

But by 1918 the railways were exhausted – both track and trains were in desperate need of maintenance and many ancient locomotives, anachronisms even in 1914, were still retained. Many of the companies were in a poor state, too: the war had robbed much of their core business, and in the new post-war world army surplus lorries began to encroach on their territory. The government was now faced with a choice: support a privately owned system or nationalise it. Formal nationalisation was generally felt to be too expensive, and for three years after the end of the war an uneasy status quo existed.

Then, in a decision typical of government involvement in the railways, it compromised, partially reorganising the system to group the existing companies into four new entities. (At one stage, parliament had even considered forming six groups rather than four. This would have allowed Scottish railways to become completely autonomous and would have created a merger of former enemies the Midland and Great Central Railways.)

This at least allowed railway companies to remain in private hands, although a certain amount of government supervision restricted their complete independence. The authorities planned to abolish competition between the different railway companies to allow a unified, if not completely co-ordinated, series of movements. The entire railway system would be rationalised, and ticketing and charging procedures standardised amongst the former rivals. The through ticketing in particular worked surprisingly smoothly; there are many who remember those times and despair over today's fragmented railway. Inevitably not all of this proposed action happened, but it kept the main players in check, effectively keeping them aware of the threat that the network might be fully nationalised at some future date.

This drastic review and re-organisation came as a wake-up call to many in the industry, persuading the key players that they must quickly become more cost-effective, or fail. It ensured that they regulated themselves more efficiently, lest they risk further intervention or a later cap-in-hand appeal for essential funding and support. Certain railway companies were forced to raise their game, regarding passengers in particular. While some expresses and first class carriages were genuinely good, many trains were slow and uncomfortable. Until new rolling stock was built, the industry had to provide a better service than the third-class standards they usually offered.

Speed, comfort and reliability soon became essential qualities in the battle amongst this new set of rivals. Yet at the same time railway operators everywhere faced competition and loss of revenue from other growing forms of passenger transport, including motor vehicles, coaches and even ocean liners. The newly developed aeroplane and airships, too, clearly had great potential. There was no room for complacency.

The original proposal, endorsed by the 1921 Railways Act, agreed a deal for the future survival of the 'Big Four', and was programmed to last for the next twenty-five years. It officially came into effect from 1 January 1923. The new agreement heralded the formation of the London and North Eastern Railway (LNER), London Midland and Scottish Railway (LMS), Great Western Railway (GWR) and Southern Railway (SR).

The Great Northern Railway was one of the seven larger companies to come within the new LNER operation; the others were the North Eastern, Great Eastern, Great Central, Hull & Barnsley, North British and Great North of Scotland Railways, along with twenty smaller outfits. The LMS incorporated twenty-seven of the old companies, the GWR twenty-six, and the SR fourteen.

A board of directors was formed and William Whitelaw appointed as first chairman of the new London and North Eastern Railway Company. Whitelaw was an MP, a wealthy landowner and an industrialist, and also a member of the General Assembly of the Church of Scotland. He had been previously been a chairman of the Highland Railway and was the chairman of the North British Railway Company at the time of the grouping. He had a fierce reputation for Scottish pride and liked to travel as much as possible, getting to know his staff, and flying the flag for the company. He became an excellent, if eccentric, ambassador. Whitelaw soon made use of the new LNER inspection coach to pass his eye over as many stations as possible, encouraging staff to take a pride in their work and in their company. In later years, he was instrumental in promoting a popular in-house competition for the best-kept station and gardens.

Another key appointment in the LNER network was the new chief general manager, Ralph Lewis Wedgwood, who had come from the North Eastern Railway (and who gained a knighthood shortly after his appointment). Wedgwood, a graduate in classics from Cambridge University, had been the first traffic apprentice on the NER management scheme – later adopted by LNER. Following the amalgamation, he wasted no time in recruiting the services of his former assistant, Robert Bell, a fellow university graduate, who, like Whitelaw, was another amiable Scot. Bell had also held a similar posting with his previous employers.

Wedgwood played a major role in a host of important business decisions, most notably securing the services of the crucial managers who would run the new company. One of the first tasks facing the newly formed LNER in 1923 was that of selecting the chief mechanical engineer, who would develop the new generation of locomotives and coaching stock needed for the coming years, and who would also be able to unify a hotch-potch of varying designs. Whoever got the job would be responsible for around 7,400 locomotives of all sorts of shapes and sizes, some with right-hand drive, others with left, some with air brakes, others with vacuum brakes, some masters of their tasks, others not. Most were very, very old.

There were three main rivals for the post. First was Sir Vincent Raven of the North Eastern Railway, an experienced engineer who had designed a successful fleet of locomotives for the stretch of line from York to Newcastle. Then came the sixty-seven-year-old CME of the Great Central Railway, John Robinson. Responsible for some of the most beautiful locomotives ever to take to the rails, he had also designed a heavy freight locomotive ordered in huge quantities during the First World War, which had proved strong, reliable and almost indestructible. Last of the contenders was the CME of the Great Northern Railway, Nigel Gresley. By this time Gresley had started to introduce some really modern designs to the company that looked set to handle not only the current traffic, but that expected for some years ahead.

The board of directors faced a difficult decision with three such able people competing for one job. It was made easier when Robinson decided not to take the job and put forward Gresley's name instead. The board, after deliberation, agreed, and installed the younger man at the helm. Raven was said to have been so devastated by the rejection that he emigrated to Australia. Gresley had not taken his posting for granted. His rivals claimed he had taken every possible opportunity to climb the promotional ladder. They criticised his reluctance to wait for 'dead men's shoes' and some even said he was arrogant. In the same breath, though, all agreed that Gresley had a persuasive manner and that he generally got what he wanted. At forty-seven, he was the youngest CME of the Big Four.

The re-organisation came at the perfect time for Gresley, who can be compared to a modern-day football manager. Appointed by the chairman, board and chief general manager, he already had a track record of success, had built a winning team, and was now ideally placed to re-sign his star performers and advance to a higher division. Gresley's work was already well known but he also carried some baggage and was regarded in some quarters as something of a controversial character. It was said that he was 'often challenged but always respected'.

To say that the man chosen to take charge of designing, building and maintaining the new LNER's vast fleet of locomotives, carriages and wagons faced a demanding task is an understatement. When Gresley took on his new role in February 1923 he inherited a variety of staff forming a veritable army of more than 100,000, stretching from facilities as far apart as the Thames and the Moray Firth. His responsibilities included twelve major workshops, more than 7,000 locomotives, 21,000 coaches, and a vast assortment of wagons, utility vehicles, road vehicles, plant, general machinery and dock equipment. This was a big job – but the LNER's board was confident it had found its man. How well placed that confidence would turn out to be would become apparent over the next seventeen years.

Gresley was the ideal man to help develop the London and North Eastern Railway network: he had the experience, the foresight and the passion to take it forward. Sir Ralph Wedgwood needed a man of vision and someone tough enough to make hard decisions. Both men knew the rolling stock needed a complete overhaul and that there was limited finance available with which to achieve it. At this stage it was more a case of making do and adapting minor adjustments and improvements to existing stock than creating revolutionary new designs.

But Gresley was well aware of the urgent need to construct new locomotives and equipment, and fully understood the desperate challenge ahead. He was determined to succeed, determined to stamp his own authority on the industry and equally determined to put the LNER on the map. He was also shrewd enough to realise that any success could make him a household name and, to a sceptical public, permanently brand his trains. In 1923 Gresley must have felt he was on the right track with his first big locomotive. Built the year before, *Great Northern* would set the scene for all that was to follow – including the sublime *Mallard*.

However good Gresley was (and he was very good), he would never have achieved his later exalted status without a superb team behind him. Perhaps his most inspired appointment was his long-standing deputy and associate, Oliver Bulleid, as principal technical assistant. Bulleid had been born at Invercargill, New Zealand, in 1882. He first joined the Great Northern Railway as a premium apprentice on a four-year scheme in January 1901 under Henry Ivatt and later became personal assistant to Webster in the locomotive running department, then to Francis Wintour, the Doncaster works manager. After several years, however, Bulleid became restless, and at the end of 1907, he left to join Westinghouse's branch in France, first as a test engineer, then chief draughtsman, and finally as assistant works manager at their Freinville works, near Paris. At the time, Gresley warned the young engineer that 'it was easy enough to leave the railway, but much more difficult to get back'.

But by December 1911 Bulleid's work was completed and he returned to Britain, looking for work back on the railways. The following year he became Gresley's personal assistant, a fortuitous appointment. Gresley and Bulleid had tremendous respect for each other and both were still relatively young, ambitious and eager to learn. They formed a unique partnership that was to last for more than three decades.

The only break in Bulleid's spell of service was a period of secondment back in France during the Great War. He volunteered for active service and was appointed to the Service Corps and commissioned as lieutenant, later working as a railway transport officer at St Omer. As the war progressed, he gained promotion to captain, then major, and became deputy assistant director of railway traffic. His supervisory work took him near the front lines and he later told of many lucky escapes, including the time he was sitting in the second coach of a train moving up towards the front, when a German shell scored a direct hit on the smokebox of the locomotive. Fortunately, he escaped unhurt; others were not so lucky. His operations included moving 15-inch heavy guns close to the German lines. They often attracted artillery fire from the enemy as the exhaust from the engines could be spotted by enemy observers for miles. His position came under heavy bombardment and, once again, he was fortunate to escape. Following this scare, he recommended an urgent re-adjustment to the exhaust extractor on the engines, pointing them downwards to avoid future detection by the enemy.

When his war duties were completed, he almost ended up in Brazil rather than back with Gresley in Doncaster. Oliver Bury, the general manager of the Great Northern, who was then controlling the São Paulo railway in Brazil, wanted Bulleid as his chief mechanical engineer. Fortunately, for Gresley and for the future of the yet-undreamt-of *Mallard*, that particular scheme was cancelled, and in February 1919, Bulleid finally secured his release from the Army and returned to Gresley's circle, where they worked closely together until the grouping took them both to London. Gresley was always considered the strong man with the firm judgement, while Bulleid was the ideas man. He respected Gresley for the fine job of organising the carriage workshops and particularly for the way he speeded up repair work and reduced costs.

Within weeks, Gresley had assembled a very experienced and reliable team. He took with him several key workers hand-picked from the staff at his old Doncaster office, including Bert Spencer, who worked as a locomotive engineer and as his specialist technical assistant. Other Great Northern men included A.E. Beresford, a clerk from Gorton works, who moved to London at Gresley's request and whose skill with languages came in extremely useful, particularly for Gresley and Bulleid's work with the International Railway Congress.

Edward Thompson, the son-in-law and former subordinate of the rejected applicant to Gresley's job, Sir Vincent Raven, soon joined the company as carriage and wagon superintendent. A tall and rather dour individual who came to the LNER from the North Eastern Railway, Thompson had first worked with Raven at the Woolwich Arsenal in 1916 and during the First World War transferred to the Directorate of Transportation in France with the rank of lieutenant colonel. He left Doncaster works in 1920 and returned to the North Eastern Railway as carriage and wagon works manager at York before moving to the LNER for the beginning of a long association with Gresley. Some critics said he finally inflicted some slight revenge on behalf of his father-in-law many years later when he eventually took over from Gresley and was responsible for a massive restructuring programme which, according to the enthusiast press, saw many classic Gresley designs horribly disfigured.

Another key appointment was Leslie Parker Preston, who became one of Gresley's most notable lieutenants. Many have claimed he was one of the most outstanding 'running men' of his generation. Preston was a former Great Eastern apprentice who quickly progressed into the works running department and at thirty-seven was appointed district locomotive superintendent at

Stratford. Always smartly dressed and sporting a bow tie, Preston was a 'tough task master' who ruled the departments with an iron rod. He drove all the staff very hard and was particularly interested in examining the reasons for any train delays. He later gained respect from within many engine sheds nationwide by supporting Gresley's personal belief that drivers should retain their own locomotives wherever possible, and encouraged them to develop a pride and interest in their work, as well as cultivating reliability. It was said of him that he never had to raise his voice and that he feared no one.

All was set for Gresley to further his revolutionary designs, except for one small problem: the LNER had little money for the new locomotives and carriages it so desperately needed.

Faced with the stark reality of a worsening internal financial crisis, combined with other worrying national and economic problems, Sir Ralph Wedgwood, the LNER's chief general manager, set about constructing a new marketing image for the company. He formed a special committee and in spring 1923 quickly re-organised the company into three main divisions covering the southern, north-eastern and Scottish regions. Each had their own general manager and was responsible to the chief general manager, whose new office was now established at King's Cross with Gresley.

Nigel Gresley naturally played an important part in this process, as did William Teasdale, Wedgwood's new advertising manager from the former North Eastern Railway. Already by 1923, Gresley had provided the first of a new generation of locomotives, and his carriages, too, were among the best running anywhere at the time. The problem the LNER now faced was how to build business so that Gresley could have a full head of steam to provide the new motive power the company so desperately needed. It succeeded triumphantly, with a superb, sustained marketing campaign that provided the justification and the wherewithal for what was to follow in the engineering department.

Teasdale already had an excellent reputation and was thoroughly experienced in modern marketing techniques. The new LNER marketing department was – like its new locomotives – very different from that of railway convention and promoted a host of innovative operations and services. Wedgwood allowed Teasdale full control and from the beginning was determined to stamp out any argumentative or competitive elements brought about by the grouping, instead encouraging employees, whichever company they came from, to unite in harmony.

From the beginning, Teasdale's approach to advertising was striking and innovative. He is best remembered for the graceful and impressionistic posters he commissioned – icons of design then and now – that depicted places of interest on the LNER routes and promoted Gresley's exciting new locomotives and running stock. He soon recognised that one of the company's most successful posters was also one of its oldest: that of the popular East Coast resort town of Skegness, designed by John Hassall of the GNR in 1907. Hassall had created a happy, carefree image of the 'Jolly Fisherman', depicting a man skipping merrily along Skegness beach at the height of the summer. Teasdale pointed out that the fact the poster was still being used fifteen years later was a tribute to its success and promoted a similar simple ideal within his own designs, recognising that although the Skegness poster was unconventional, it continued to attract interest and still brought plenty of visitors to the seaside town. He copied the idea again years later for the Caledonian Railway, promoting the Bridge of Allan in Scotland in similar vein.

Teasdale boasted of having an artistic eye and was as determined as Wedgwood to put the LNER on the map. He chose a range of talented artists to create pictorial and informative posters, amongst them many of the top people of the day, including Austin Cooper, Frank Newbould and Tom Purvis, who went on to gain fame as one of LNER's finest illustrators. Teasdale did not suffer fools gladly and set very high standards for all his artists, yet he was very proud of his team, referring to them as his 'Big Five'.

In May 1924, Teasdale persuaded the company to establish its own press, publicity and marketing department within the advertising department. This, he argued, would keep everyone informed about future developments, including continual improvements to locomotives, carriages and standards of service, as well as providing news of any record attempts and a host of new marketing concepts. It set the template for almost all railway publicity departments that followed. His efforts were so successful that before long the other three of the Big Four companies chose to emulate the LNER's approach, imitation, of course, being the sincerest form of flattery. His talents were appreciated within the company as well, and within four years he was appointed as assistant to the general manager.

While Teasdale was revolutionising the marketing side of the railway industry, Gresley was doing the same for its engineering functions. Very much a 'hands-on' CME, Gresley was happy to attend personally to major problems whenever necessary. In his younger days, he could often be seen inspecting a locomotive or examining valve gear, dressed in a navy-blue boiler suit and a bowler hat. One day he was walking around Doncaster works when he came across a young apprentice gingerly chiselling a piece of metal. 'Give me that here,' said Gresley, and taking the tool from his hand he enthusiastically demonstrated to the young man how it should be used. Then he walked away pleased with a job well done, unaware he had ruined the poor apprentice's work.

He was noted for his marvellous memory and attention to detail; it was said he was always scribbling designs on bits of papers or even occasionally on tablecloths in restaurants. He had an idiosyncratic sense of humour and his key colleague and friend Oliver Bulleid claimed he was 'incapable of ill temper'. He was, in general, prepared to listen to other opinions and always ready, able and willing to investigate anything relating to a particular design or development. And, of course, with experience at all levels in the engineering department, he had enough knowledge and experience to come to an informed judgement should there be any debate.

One thing Gresley could not tolerate, however, was disloyalty. He demanded unremitting service and dedication and if he worked late, he expected others to follow his example. He was six years older than Bulleid and considered the latter his 'quiet assistant', saying Bulleid listened more than he talked. Bulleid was a very straight-faced and serious man, with small round-lens glasses. He had the utmost respect for his colleague, whom he considered one of the finest engineers in the country. Although they argued on occasions, Gresley relied on Bulleid's opinions before making any final decisions. Bulleid said Gresley was the best chief he ever worked under, adding: 'Our relationship was the happiest. If he agreed to try something, it would be almost certain of success.'

Other staff members were also tremendously loyal to Gresley. Many practically idolised him and kept his picture on the walls next to them for years. He himself said the men were not afraid of him but noticed how diligent and observant he was. Some claimed that during inspections Gresley always expected to be challenged – but was generally so well briefed that he could answer any question. What was Gresley like to work with? Well, he seems to have left a legacy of love and loyalty behind him at the LNER. Staff reports rarely had anything detrimental to say about him; on the contrary, despite his reputation as being a tough, ruthless and demanding engineer and manager, most still had an enviable respect and affection for him. Gresley certainly expected one hundred per cent support and loyalty, but was also known to be kind and considerate to all those who worked for him.

Many times he would meet trains as they arrived at King's Cross, or at other mainline stations, to discuss a new modification with footplate crew. It was said Gresley had an excellent grapevine to inform him of any misdemeanour, no matter how small. Once, even his friend and assistant, Oliver Bulleid, fell foul of Gresley's unique management system: Bulleid had ordered a locomotive to make an emergency stop in order to find out how quickly its engine could come to a halt. The noise was deafening: apparently trucks shunted and clattered into each other, causing general alarm and distress to a (no doubt) unprepared guard. The train managed to hold the tracks but on the following day Gresley demanded Bulleid's presence to explain matters. He warned his subordinate that the incident was a serious breach of discipline, carried out without any authority. In a gruff voice, Gresley told Bulleid it must not happen again. Bulleid hung his head low and was about to leave when Gresley asked him to sit down and tell him what the outcome had been; he was just as curious as Bulleid about the effects of a sudden stop.

Gresley's lifelong practice of 'management by walking about' inspired confidence in the running staff, since they felt their chief knew intimately what was going on. A former premium apprentice, J.H. Harrison, recalled:

My first meeting took place in his office at Doncaster, when I went to be interviewed for a position as a premium apprentice. I started in the top turnery at the plant works. I recently found a letter by Mr Gresley to my mother, saying the foreman, under whom I served my trial month, had reported I was satisfactory, therefore Mr Gresley would be pleased to accept me as a premium apprentice.

After three years' apprenticeship, I asked Mr Gresley if I could become a pupil of his, because pupillage enabled me to have training in the pattern shop, foundry, carriage works and drawing office – none of which was covered in the premium apprentice scheme. This was agreed, and in due time, on completion, I went to the locomotive running department at Doncaster, and from there to southern area headquarters at Liverpool Street.

My job was to investigate locomotive failures. Often, when I got back into King's Cross, I used to go to the messengers' office for a cup of tea. These young men looked grand in their smart uniforms. One day, the headman asked: 'Why don't you go and see Mr Gresley?' I said that I had nothing to say to him.

However, he disappeared and then soon returned saying: 'Mr G. will see you now.' Imagine my panic. Nevertheless, there was nothing for it but to go in. He asked how I was getting on and what I was doing now and then asked: 'Would you like to go back into the works? I have a vacancy at Gorton for an assistant works manager.'

I jumped at the idea and then he asked me what my salary was. I told him £325 per annum. He said: 'We'll make it £425, just wait a moment whilst I confirm this with Mr Bell.' He came back and replied: 'Mr Bell says you can only have a rise of £50 because you had a rise of £25 a little over a year ago.'

This illustrates how great a part luck plays in one's life, as Gresley had intended to settle the job that weekend and I was only the third on his list. This also shows how tight money was, not only for salaries but also for all new works, experiments and so on. Mr Gresley came to Gorton a number of times whenever there was something to interest him.

Barney Symes was another key worker and former employee of Gresley's, who worked at Doncaster for forty-three years, starting in the works as a premium apprentice. He later entered the locomotive drawing office, where he eventually retired as chief draughtsman. He said:

My first contact with Mr Gresley, as he then was, happened in 1921 when at the age of sixteen, I was summoned to present myself for an interview for a premium apprenticeship at the Doncaster works of the Great Northern Railway.

Gresley's London office was above number 10 platform at King's Cross and he personally interviewed all would-be apprentices and pupils. When I was ushered into his presence, he received me very kindly with the words, 'So you want to be a locomotive engineer, do you?'

He then proceeded to tell me not to be carried away by the glamour and that attainment of my ambition would entail a lot of hard work. I had taken along a model of a vertical steam engine that I had just completed and he gave this a thorough examination and asked how various parts were made. I do not know if this had any influence but I was told I could start the next week, and if I had no friends in Doncaster, I could apply to the local YMCA where a number of apprentices lodged. It would at least be a respectable lodging, was close to the works and would give me time to look around. I never did look around and stayed there for fifteen years!

While I often saw Gresley's imposing figure going round the works, the only point of contact was on social occasions, [such as] the annual dinner of the Doncaster Pupils and Premium Apprentices Association – which he always tried to attend.

On becoming CME of the newly formed LNER in 1923, Gresley moved his office together with the technical assistants to London, so we only saw him when he came up to see some special job, or probably just for a look around. I was transferred to the drawing office in 1930 when the V1 three-cylinder tank engine was being designed. The chief draughtsman showed me Gresley's sketch for the proposed engine on a piece of blotting paper. At least it made a change from the back of an envelope. When the first engine was completed and in steam, Gresley rode on it up and down the works yard and through the chief draughtsman, thanked us all for our efforts.

As he was no longer resident at Doncaster, it became the practice to send all important drawings to London for his approval. We did not make the finished cloth tracings ready for issuing drawings to the works until pencil tracings on thin paper had received his approval, or blue pencil, as might be the case.

On one occasion at Doncaster works, Gresley went into the paint shop, then climbed up into the cab of a Pacific, and demanded a piece of paper. On it, he sketched a device of levers to improve the safety of water gauge cocks so that both cocks were closed simultaneously if a glass burst without the driver being scalded. Gresley had been told of such an accident a day or two before and he was determined to find an immediate solution – which later became standard in all future constructions.

It was abundantly clear to all that Gresley had learned his trade the hard way. When he had gained his first premier appointment as Ivatt's successor in 1911, the forward-thinking directors had shown tremendous confidence in his ability. But it was during his time at the London and North Eastern Railway that Gresley's talents really came to the fore.

Chapter Four
The *Flying Scotsman*

Gresley's third Pacific, and the first under the LNER banner, was the A1 Pacific *Flying Scotsman*. One of Gresley's favourites, and soon equally popular with the public, it first appeared out of Doncaster in February 1923, with the works number of 1564, and a running number of 1472 (it was later renumbered as No. 4472). It cost the amazing sum of £7,944 – which doesn't sound very much now, but was a fortune then.

The locomotive was chosen to represent the company within the Palace of Engineering at the British Empire Exhibition from 23 April to 1 November 1924, and again the following year, when it was featured next to GWR's No. 4073, *Caerphilly Castle*, which its operator claimed was the most powerful locomotive in the British Isles. The Castle class designed by Charles Collett, the chief mechanical engineer of the GWR, was much smaller than the A1 but the Great Western claimed that its engines had a higher starting tractive effort, meaning they could get a heavier train moving. In response the LNER argued, not unreasonably, that sustained ability should be the deciding factor when comparing rival locomotives. The GWR's approach was rather like a car manufacturer claiming that a small but fast sports car is better than a bigger, more powerful (in horsepower terms) grand tourer. The disagreement became widely known, and the two companies' rivalry was soon a major talking point with newspapers and the public. Such was the controversy that the companies agreed to run trials against each other. Gresley's reaction to this decision is not known but he certainly had a near obsession with trials, competition and thorough investigation.

The trials were arranged in haste over two weeks from the end of May 1925. It was agreed that the locomotives would compete on the routes of both companies, the LNER line from King's Cross to Doncaster and the GWR one from Paddington to Plymouth. From the beginning, the LNER contingent fared badly. Gresley's representative, *Flying Fox*, suffered seriously on its first day with overheated bearings. It was replaced, with No. 2545, but this was hindered by other technical problems and fared little better. The LNER driver, Ben Glasgow, was heavily criticised during the trial, with some people claiming he was 'unenterprising'. He was the senior driver at King's Cross top shed at the time and some felt he was better at coping with Atlantics than with the much bigger Gresley designs. He also had a reputation for being heavy-handed, forcing the fireman to shovel more coal. A young inspector, Freddie Harrison, who accompanied Glasgow on the footplate, said he was not welcomed. It was hardly an auspicious start.

The first week consisted of preliminary trials, with the GWR engine proving a complete success on most tests. To Gresley's surprise and discomfort, it completely outshone No. 2545. During the tests, Gresley and his colleagues were astonished one day to see *Pendennis Castle* haul a 475-ton train out of King's Cross without slipping: even his own engines couldn't have performed as assuredly. He also noted that the Great Western engines were more efficient with track sanding, with their use of materials, and with the ease of use of the regulator. *Pendennis Castle* beat the bigger Gresley engines both on time and on the amount of coal burned. It looked like it was game, set and match to the Great Western.

But on the Western line, with a different driver (Albert Pibworth) and a different locomotive (No. 4474), the A1 performed much better than its fellow locomotive, soon getting used to the different coal burned on the Great Western. Despite some acute difficulties with reverse bends and gradients on the challenging south Devon sections, the A1 proved itself comfortably able to haul heavy loads up the notorious Devon gradients, bettering the GWR's speed at some points, and keeping almost perfectly to schedule.

But the overall results gave a decisive victory to the smaller Castle engines. The news generated plenty of publicity – much to Gresley's annoyance, as he had believed he had a gentleman's agreement with Charles Collett to keep the test results concealed until they were fully analysed. The results suggested that the reason for the *Castle*'s victory could be that it used the smaller amount of steam it generated more efficiently than the A1. The crucial element here was the valves used to let steam into and out of the cylinders: if the valves and their openings are too small, not enough steam can get in, whereas if they are too big then useful steam is let out before it has done its work. It was (and continues to be) something of an art form getting these proportions right.

Some claim *Pendennis Castle*'s stay on the LNER gave Gresley's men an unofficial opportunity to 'spy' on its workings, or at least examine them in secret. The story goes that his engineering staff arrived after GWR staff had left for the day and that they removed and carefully examined piston valves and other vital components. In July of the same year, rumour had it that another small team from Gresley's Doncaster plant gained a second unexpected chance to discover the Castle class's secrets when two more rival engines, *Windsor Castle* and *Viscount Churchill*, arrived for display at the Stockton & Darlington Centenary Parade and exhibitions. If the story is true, their handiwork fortunately remained undiscovered, and the rumours tell us more about the strong emotions generated by the rail companies' rivalry than anything else, since Gresley could easily have worked out the Castle's valve gear from published dimensions.

Gresley's chief technical assistant, Bert Spencer, had already put forward his own suggested designs and improvements to valve gear. Gresley had initially rejected these plans, but now he changed his mind. The working of all A1s entering the workshops was reviewed, and modifications fitted on test to A1, No. 2555, *Centenary*, along with similar essential upgrades to A3, No. 2743, *Felstead*. They included new long-lap, long-travel valve gear, which was re-tested along with narrow-ringed piston valves, making the steam flow more easily. Gresley also reviewed boiler designs and once again considered increasing the steam pressure, since he realised that part of the GWR's success was the result of the higher working pressure used in their boilers – 225psi against his own 180psi. Subsequently Gresley increased the pressure used in his boilers to the GWR level, and also adopted GWR-type long-lap piston valves.

Fortunately for Gresley's team, his revised tests proved a great success and the experimental locomotives were extremely efficient, recording some excellent performances. Gresley even travelled on the footplate of one particular locomotive to finally convince himself that the new modifications worked satisfactorily, and he later ordered similar refinements to the rest of the A1 class. A useful side effect of the modifications was that not only did the altered engines perform better, they also used less coal, which made further rebuilding easier to justify to the accountants. The results led to the development of the A3 – an A1 with all the modifications Gresley decided on – and other future Pacifics, which were designed for high-speed passenger working. Between August 1927 and February 1935, Gresley produced twenty-seven new A3s. The standard was set.

As time was to prove, Gresley's A3s were powerful and fast enough to power East Coast Main Line expresses for many years. And Gresley himself was becoming famous; in July 1925, he hosted a royal visit from the Duke and Duchess of York to the Railway Centenary Exhibition at Darlington and noted the royal couple's particular interest in the lathe once owned by railway inventor George Stephenson. Many engineers would now be thinking about putting their feet up or perhaps concentrating on other things. However, Gresley's desire for innovation was awakened afresh by a new approach to marketing which promised to expand business still further and stimulate customer expectations, which in turn would need to be matched by further developments in railway technology.

The LNER press and publicity chief William Teasdale had moved on, and his successor was another excellent marketing man, Cecil Dandridge, who began work at King's Cross on 1 January 1927. Like Gresley's deputy, Oliver Bulleid, Dandridge had also worked for the traffic office of the army in France. He too became a major, and in 1917 Dandridge was in charge of traffic for the Archangel Northern Railway in Russia, where he met the beautiful Princess Olga Gallitzin. When his work was finished, she returned with him to England, where they were married.

In 1927, the marketing department was attached to the chief general manager's office of Sir Ralph Wedgwood, and Dandridge was originally called an 'information agent'. At the time, LNER was spending enormous amounts of money on advertising in certain preferred newspapers and the board decided to separate marketing from the purchase of advertising space, and gain as much free publicity as possible by persuading journalists to highlight the LNER's latest achievements in news stories. At the same time, Dandridge persuaded the board and each manager of the various railway companies to run joint operations regarding advertising. By November 1927, he had secured the co-operation of all concerned. He saw this as a major step forward in overall marketing terms and one which would save the company both time and money.

Dandridge was also keen to improve the visual appearance of the company logos and all its printed material. He was a friend of the well-known artist and sculptor Eric Gill, who was also a talented graphic designer. Dandridge asked Gill to produce a unique new typeface. The artist gave it much thought and experimentation before submitting an unconventional new design he christened 'Gill Sans', which Dandridge persuaded the LNER board to use throughout the company, effectively creating a unique branding for all their products and services. By 1932 the new typeface appeared on posters, timetables, leaflets and all company documents, even on station noticeboards, tickets and posters, and the public soon came to associate it with the LNER.

However, a problem that had troubled first Teasdale, and now Dandridge, was that a good section of the public still thought of the railways as they had been in 1844: dark, dour and dingy. The railways had been fondly termed the 'chief national amusement' by the press (how little things have changed since!) and Dandridge, the board and other senior officials were keen to alter this. The LNER management insisted the network should run smoothly and efficiently, and wanted the publicity department to project the right image. They decided to make punctuality a key marketing tool: railway guards received large pocket watches and giant clocks gradually appeared on platforms and at all mainline stations.

By the late 1920s, the publicity department had become acutely aware that most stations were bland and boring – but that they possessed vast possibilities in terms of unused space. So the company logo and its new typeface were prominently displayed throughout stations, and Dandridge encouraged his artists to design a series of colourful posters that could run side by side, creating a more interesting and exciting environment – and also covering any unsightly gaps. These posters advertised holiday resorts in scenic locations on the LNER railway network. It was all part of a marketing process, designed to open the public's minds to the various destinations on offer and encourage people to travel as widely as possible – preferably booking their holidays with the LNER.

Competition from other modes of transport was still fierce,

with massive rival advertisements from motor coach companies, touring cars, airlines and ocean liners. This second-wave poster campaign for the LNER proved a success but others soon started using similar methods to attract customers. Dandridge, always ready with new ideas, hastened to invent several other unique marketing ideas to keep the LNER name before the public. These included hiring out slides to clubs, societies and colleges to promote tourist areas and places of interest for group bookings. By 1929, the slides were very much in demand, with sixteen different sets available and about 1500 out on loan at any one time. The LNER arranged holiday packages, ran hotels and ferries, and even supplied special camping coaches. They took the opportunity to show locomotives, trains and even drivers' faces on miscellaneous items, and featured maps of the famous journeys taken by the likes of the 'Flying Scotsman' (and, later, 'Coronation') passenger expresses.

LNER express drivers became almost as famous as today's football stars. The company also promoted paperweights, scale models, commemorative plates and playing cards, mostly made by John Waddington of Leeds. In total, the manufacturers produced more than fifty different packs of pictorial cards between 1925 and 1939. Many included scenes of famous places or railway journeys. They also produced the Monopoly game and other travelling board games such as snakes and ladders – all based on LNER railway themes. One London store, Gamages, even used LNER platform equipment, posters and uniforms to create a special Christmas display based on the Silver Jubilee in 1935.

Another vital ingredient in LNER's increasing public prominence was the growth of model railways. The Germans had been the first to capitalise on this idea in the late 1800s, when toy makers began making wooden replicas. Märklin produced a superb figure-of-eight track with a small train, then, twenty years later, another rival German firm, Bing, produced a wooden tabletop train set. Now the idea spread to Britain, with Hornby producing a wide range of models which before long became the must-have present for children's birthdays and Christmas. Some of the LNER's famous locomotives were recreated as models, which even displayed minute LNER logos, again helping promote and maintain the brand image.

The LNER was always keen on any free publicity and looked after journalists who looked after them with favourable articles. Many national media representatives were encouraged to travel on speed test trials. The press were also introduced to several of the Gresley team's new ideas and developments, including a cinema car, new restaurant facilities, headphone sets with music and news, and hairdressing salons. As early as March 1924 some enjoyed a special excursion when, seated in unique and rather uncomfortable bucket seats, they were shown Pathé news clips in a travelling cinema. The press were also shown Gresley's radical design for tilting trains – about six decades before Sir Richard Branson first considered the idea – though sadly it never came to pass.

The press were often alerted to new plans well in advance: Dandridge knew that an innovative idea was likely to gain national press coverage and he knew how to manipulate and stimulate the press, realising that they could create additional interest and thus boost passenger traffic. The LNER was keen to retain its popular and flamboyant public image and often invited reporters to share and enjoy first-class hospitality.

In addition to promoting Gresley's latest ideas, Dandridge also helped organise a series of other exciting promotional challenges, featuring well-known personalities competing in races using different modes of transport. Just after the *Flying Scotsman*'s first non-stop run was announced in May 1928, Dandridge arranged a promotional trip in conjunction with fellow publicity seekers Imperial Airways. Most of the press flew with Captain Gordon Olley, the rest travelled on the *Scotsman*. The plan was to meet at the Royal Border Bridge, Berwick, and then again later at

Edinburgh Waverley station. However, the pilot became distract-
ed pointing out to reporters various landmarks en route and
missed the rendezvous at Berwick. Realising his mistake, he
quickly continued to Edinburgh but again missed the train by
only a few minutes. A couple of years later, another race was
organised between air, land and water. One party travelled along
the River Ouse in a speedboat for a distance of three miles
against the LNER express, hauled by No. 2549, *Persimmon*, and a
light aircraft. Surprisingly, the train travelling at just 80mph won,
largely owing to unexpected navigational problems experienced
by the other two competitors.

Rivals at the GWR and elsewhere were again quick to follow
suit with similar marketing gimmicks (such as the famous London, Midland and Scottish Railways ashtrays) as well as copying
several other key projects. But the LNER steamed ahead:
between 1924 and 1937 it produced some forty-three different
puzzles, and even ran a competition asking customers how long it
had taken them to complete them, offering various incentives for
prompt replies. Dandridge was keen to gauge public perception
of his work, seeing it as an important step in customer
interaction.

One of LNER's finest marketing weapons was the 'Flying Scotsman' express, by then one of the most famous trains in the
world. The locomotive named after it soon became as famous as
the train itself, with its image appearing on biscuit tins, puzzles
and posters all over the world, a dream for the LNER publicity
department (and now for that of the National Railway Museum
in York, where it is based today).

The northbound express departed each weekday morning at
precisely 10 a.m. from Platform 10 at King's Cross station,
bound for Scotland; the southbound express left Edinburgh
Waverley at the same time for London. It was a routine that had
run like clockwork since the service had first begun in June

1862. In the early days, the train consisted of just seven coaches weighing 265 tons, but over the years both the quality of the rolling stock and the demand for seats had improved considerably. At the height of its success the train consisted of at least fourteen carriages, with a load of some 450 tons — a massive load for a passenger train. During the busy summer periods, this load sometimes increased to between 500 and 600 tons. Because of the sheer power required, following the grouping in 1923 the LNER began to use Pacifics to haul the express, sometimes the *Flying Scotsman* locomotive itself. Some portions of the train continued to Perth, Glasgow and Aberdeen; LNER revealed, with a typical flair for publicity, that the distance the service covered between the various points in London and Scotland each year was enough to take the train around the world five times.

When the 'Scotsman' service first started, there were no corridor carriages and no restaurant facilities. Until 1900, the train stopped at York for twenty minutes, while passengers hastily ate their lunch in the station dining room. When restaurant cars were eventually added, this meal break was reduced to a ten-minute 'comfort stop'. In later years, the train became something of a travelling hotel, with luxurious hairdressing salons for men and women, a cocktail bar, ladies' room and a richly furnished, state-of-the-art restaurant car with electric kitchens, hot water, double-glazing and electricity. The train declared its famous name on the front of the engine's smokebox with a white name board and black lettering. The coaches, too, carried similar identification on both sides of the roof of each coach, and in large letters on the rear of the last coach. Complete with beautiful varnished teak-bodied coaches with white roofs, the express became a quick, convenient and luxurious way of travelling. All services were well advertised and marketed, and often the trains were fully booked well in advance.

The 'Flying Scotsman' was the train that would cement Nigel Gresley's place in engineering history. In 1927, with more of his successful Pacifics running, the service was so busy that an extra 'relief' train had to be put on during the height of the summer season, running non-stop from King's Cross to Newcastle, a distance of 268.3 miles. It was a remarkable effort, but Gresley had his eye on an even more impressive first: a non-stop run from London to Edinburgh. To achieve this, the LNER would rely on the aid of another incredible Gresley invention: the corridor tender.

The tender hauled behind a steam locomotive was designed to carry coal and water. The water could be topped up from troughs laid between the rails at strategic points on the route, and the tender could be made big enough to carry sufficient coal. The limiting factor was the crew – shovelling for perhaps seven hours at a time without much of a break was exhausting work for the fireman, and beyond the limits of reasonable endurance. There was usually a change of driver and fireman at Newcastle, but if the train was to run non-stop from London to Edinburgh this would not be possible, so some means of getting a fresh crew from the train to the locomotive was needed.

Gresley's brainwave was to incorporate a narrow corridor about five feet high by eighteen inches wide along the side of the tender, which would allow crews to move between the locomotive and the train behind. The crew would then be able to change over at the midway point of the journey – generally somewhere near Alne, about eleven miles from York. Testing his theory at home one weekend, Gresley carefully positioned his dining chairs at the right width and crawled through the gap to prove his idea would work. His children must have thought he'd gone mad, but the episode illustrates an important point about Gresley's character: he was unwilling to impose on his crews a concept as bizarre as a corridor tender without making sure it would work first.

The first corridor tender was built in absolute secrecy in Doncaster: under no account was the LNER's great rival, the London, Midland and Scottish Railway, to hear of it. The tender was huge, with a capacity of 5000 gallons of water and about nine tons of coal. The corridor was dimly lit by a small circular window and by the fire from the firebox. In total, the tender weighed a staggering 56 tons. During trials before its unveiling, it was being hauled by an Ivatt Atlantic (to reduce the chance of anyone guessing its purpose) when the driver found himself unexpectedly stopped near Retford, despite having been promised a clear road ahead. At the signalbox, the driver asked why he'd been held: 'Oh, you've got a clear road all right,' said the signalman. 'I just wanted to take a look at your new corridor tender.' The railway grapevine proved impossible to silence, then as now, but somehow the secret was kept from the public.

Gresley's Pacifics were such a triumph that hundreds of enthusiasts packed the platform at King's Cross just to catch a glimpse of them. On 1 May 1928 the train was hauled by A1 Pacific, No. 4472, the *Flying Scotsman* itself, driven by Albert Pibworth from the Gateshead shed – the same man who had excelled for Gresley in earlier steam trials against the GWR. Much to the joy of Gresley and his colleagues at the LNER, their hopes were fulfilled: the *Flying Scotsman* ran non-stop from London to Edinburgh and took the world non-stop steam record from the GWR.

Gresley began to introduce his revolutionary tenders to the route, eventually reducing the overall journey time to 7 hours and 30 minutes. The 'Flying Scotsman' became so popular that passenger numbers doubled between 1923 and 1938, and the LNER's new weapon proved a stunning success right up until the end of steam. It has been claimed the success of these tenders prompted another idea: an observation chamber at the front of the tender to allow favoured passengers to watch the enginemen at work. But it's doubtful whether Gresley was responsible for this proposal, which went no further. His achievements had been quite dramatic enough already.

Chapter Five
Developments across the Channel

Professionally Gresley could not have been more successful, but his home life was less happy. In the late 1920s, the health of his wife Ethel began to give cause for concern. Diagnosed with cancer, she underwent a serious operation at the family home. Her dressing room was converted into a makeshift operating theatre and, although she made an initial recovery, her health soon deteriorated. The surgeon, Sir Maurice Cassidy, told Gresley that her condition was terminal. Ethel Gresley died on 5 August 1929, aged fifty-four, and was buried in the family graveyard at Netherseale, in Derbyshire, under a Boscobel oak. Her death came as a major blow to her family and particularly to Gresley himself; some of his colleagues believed he never fully recovered from the shock.

Struggling to come to terms with the loss, Gresley was persuaded to take a holiday in Canada with his elder daughter, Violet, known as Vi. They travelled to the Rocky Mountains, where supporters hoped the bracing air would revive his spirits. Then they stayed at Banff for a few weeks, where they were occasionally entertained by friends and staff from the Canadian Pacific Railway. Gresley even travelled on the footplate of a massive CPR 2-10-4 locomotive during a trip to Glacier in British Columbia, and later wrote about his exploits in the *Railway Gazette*.

His visit coincided with the dramatic Wall Street crash of 1929 and perhaps this shortened their trip. When Gresley returned to England, he first moved to London's Cadogan Square and later to a historic house with a moat, Salisbury Hall, near St Albans. It was here that he first developed an interest in the breeding of wild birds and ducks, and where he fell in love with his favourite species – the mallard. It was the name he would chose for his famous train. Gresley stayed at Salisbury Hall for several years until Vi, to whom he was obviously very close, set up home with her husband, engineer Geoffrey Godfrey, at Watton-on-Stone; Gresley left his beloved Salisbury Hall to live with them.

Despite Gresley's personal grief, he continued to generate new ideas for improving locomotive performance. The Wall Street crash, coupled with a lack of firm policies to help the country recover from the Great War, started the ripples of a deep recession in Britain. Raw materials were becoming more expensive, and fuel efficiency was becoming a hot issue.

The matter was already in the air in 1926, just as the A1s were starting to prove themselves, when a fortuitous meeting organised by a colleague of Nigel Gresley's led to a remarkable association. André Chapelon was a promising young French engineer who was being hailed as something of a genius in Europe: his modifications to some ageing steam locomotives had achieved spectacular results. A technical director at Davey Paxman, a specialist firm in Colchester who were the licensed agents for supplying patents of a new design of valve gear, had invited Chapelon to England to review the various products needed for the rebuilding of a French locomotive. This director also happened to know Nigel Gresley well and thought the two men might benefit from mutual discussions. He was also aware of Chapelon's extensive research and experiments with the American railway network – another interest of Gresley's. Chapelon and Gresley met at a London hotel and got on like a house on fire: they soon became the best of friends.

Born in October 1892 at Saint Paul, Cornillon, in the Loire, Chapelon spoke fluent English, and even had some British blood. He was the great-grandson of a former Sheffield forge master, James Jackson, who had travelled to France in 1812 to teach new steel production techniques, and remained there. Chapelon was the chief mechanical engineer of the Paris–Orleans Railway and, like Gresley, one of the few CMEs actively involved in experimental design work. Chapelon shared Gresley's habit of scribbling potential design ideas on scraps of paper or the backs of envelopes, or even on white linen tablecloths in restaurants.

Fondly nicknamed 'Le Petit' or 'Shorty' by friends and colleagues, the Frenchman was one of the brightest locomotive engineers and specialists in the world since Robert Stephenson. Unlike Gresley, though, he was a serious man with a rather glum expression, short and stocky, with a chubby face. He had a broad moustache and was smart and well dressed, preferring dark suits, and wore a wide-brimmed hat. Chapelon had a very matter-of-fact manner and could not stand time wasters. He examined every problem in a scientific manner and supporters claimed he could accurately predict some extraordinary results from his tests. For two decades, beginning in the early 1920s, he helped make considerable improvements to French rolling stock considered by many to be past its best. His modifications were aimed at getting the best use of the coal being burned and the water being boiled in a steam locomotive. Where previously internal steam pipes had awkward angles, he smoothed the curves to make it as easy as possible for the steam to reach the cylinders, and, by altering the exhaust, he was able to make the fire burn hotter, generating more steam to go through the revised pipes. His modifications were simple to adapt and highly fuel-efficient – but, most importantly, they offered a simple and cheap way of dramatically improving the performance of steam locomotives. It's no wonder Gresley was so interested in his work.

Chapelon favoured modern scientific techniques to test his theories and preferred using locomotives on genuine work trials. Few engineers had as much technical or scientific experience, yet his work was often better known overseas than in France, and many believed he failed to receive the recognition he deserved in his own country. Chapelon used innovative ideas never before seen in Europe, including the use of high-speed stroboscopic cameras to study the flow of steam. He was also the first person to successfully apply compounding to locomotives, re-using high-pressure steam leaving small cylinders to power larger, low-pressure cylinders. This technique had been used for decades in ships, but the lack of space in a locomotive made its application difficult.

He also helped develop the Kylchap exhaust system, which speeds up the flow of hot gases leaving the chimney, thus causing more to be drawn through the boiler tubes and heating the water faster, developing his own particular design shape in the process. This design was later used extensively in Gresley's Pacific constructions. The Frenchman designed some of the most powerful locomotives in the world for their weight, and some were in a class of their own regarding economy and fuel efficiency, even occasionally beating more modern electric locomotives.

Chapelon shared Gresley's fascination with American rolling stock. In particular, they regularly discussed the results of detailed tests concerning high-performance Mikado-class engines running on the New York Central line, and several others on Chicago's Great Western system. Chapelon carefully examined the performances of a number of successful American types to discover how they performed so well. The Frenchman became almost obsessed with his findings and later incorporated many American design factors within his own productions and experiments, believing that the overseas emphasis was 'more geared to achieving power through high-steam output with a high-capacity boiler; as opposed to maximising power by minimising steam consumption'.

Chapelon's 4-6-2 designs, and his highly rated 4-8-0s of 1931, were thought to be some of the most powerful locomotives in Europe. His 4-8-0s greatly impressed Gresley and Bulleid, and several other highly respected international mechanical engineers. The design incorporated several key features, including

Kylchap exhaust, steel firebox (easier and cheaper to build and maintain than the typical copper firebox), and several modifications to the steam passage system that were later considered for use by Gresley in his famous Pacific designs.

It was primarily thanks to the association between Chapelon and Gresley that Gresley developed the so-called 'hush-hush' compound locomotive No. 10000, built in secret at Darlington in 1929. Speculation had built up throughout the summer that the LNER was in the process of developing a revolutionary new steam locomotive, which would supposedly include many new modifications based on Gresley's overseas research. Nobody could have predicted just how different this 'hush-hush' locomotive would be.

After months of secrecy, compound test engine No. 10000 was finally revealed on 10 December 1929. Its design was spectacular but Gresley played down its precise role, announcing that it was built to examine fuel efficiency and that it was neither powerful nor speedy. The engine had a unique high-pressure boiler and unconventional chimney, and arrived complete with a new corridor tender almost identical to that of the *Flying Scotsman* from the previous May. Like its counterpart, the locomotive was intended for use on the London to Edinburgh route.

However, when No. 10000 first came into service, it was primarily used between York and King's Cross. It also worked the Scottish route on occasion, proving that it was both strong and quick, and gaining plaudits for its performance on the non-stop 'Flying Scotsman' service to Edinburgh.

The locomotive was displayed at many exhibitions nationally and at several LNER open days. It became a magnificent publicity product and frequently ran with the dynamometer car used to measure speed accurately, becoming a star attraction at various events, including railwaymen's charities. Unfortunately, it proved unreliable in regular service. Gresley discussed performance problems with Chapelon, who suggested fitting the double

Kylchap exhaust and a superheater to help overcome condensation problems in the lower boiler. But following a period of extensive testing, Gresley admitted that No. 10000 had not lived up to expectations: serious problems had been identified during maintenance and fuel consumption was far greater than anticipated.

No. 10000 was finally withdrawn from service in August 1935, and spent over a year in sidings at Darlington before it was returned to Doncaster works to be rebuilt with a conventional boiler and new streamlined casing. Rebuilt, it was the largest passenger locomotive ever to run in the British Isles. Only then did it finally prove its worth by hauling some exceptionally heavy passenger trains on the route between Edinburgh and Newcastle. However, it was still considered uneconomical because of its high maintenance costs.

1929 had proved a dramatic year for Gresley, combining public success with private sorrow and with technical innovation on an impressive scale. By this time Gresley had become the country's most famous railwayman, and an ambassador for Britain's railways at home and abroad. From 1927 onwards, he advocated the development in England of a static locomotive testing plant, where full component analysis and experiments could be conducted in a scientific manner. Only limited facilities were available in the UK at that time. There was the GWR's test plant at Swindon, plus four dynamometer cars which could be hauled behind a locomotive to measure performance. Gresley pointed out that the Americans had authorised a new pioneer plant at Altoona by the Pennsylvania Railroad Company, and that the Europeans, too, had realised the potential benefits of having their own unique facilities, agreeing to build a national test centre under Chapelon's supervision in France. Both plants were partially funded by generous government sponsorship and Gresley felt the British were rapidly being left behind. A national testing plant would advance efficiency and performance of locomotives

– and would have exposed No. 10000's flaws before it saw service. In a passionate address to the Institution of Locomotive Engineers in 1927, Gresley called for a test plant and experimental station for engines.

Gresley's proposals were supported by a Board of Trade committee in June 1930, but, owing to the economic climate, they were rejected. In July 1931, he was still pushing for a testing plant, and he and other British CMEs joined forces. They accused the government of a lack of initiative, foresight and investment; in the main the country relied upon individual railway companies to develop their own facilities and invest their own money. Gresley proposed plans to develop a site at Cross Gates near Leeds and later at a plant near Rugby. He even spoke about the urgent need for these test facilities to Winston Churchill, who had served as Chancellor of the Exchequer in the late 1920s but was now out of office, and also argued for the need for government sponsorship to help develop and standardise locomotives. But nothing came to pass. The issue became a sore point with Gresley and he remained furious for many years at what he saw as a grave omission.

The refusal to build a testing plant was not the only example of the British government failing to develop its railway services. On 5 June 1930, the government rejected an ambitious plan to construct a Channel Tunnel which would have catered for both road and rail services. A pilot entrance had been constructed and preparation work at Dover completed, but the scheme was not considered feasible by MPs, who wished to protect the country's independence. This was a disappointment for the LNER; in the old Great Central route, the company possessed the only main line in the country with big enough clearances to allow larger European trains to operate, and running services directly from England to the continent would have given the company an excellent opportunity to expand profitably.

But Gresley did not stop having ideas. From May 1932, the journey time of the 'Flying Scotsman' to Edinburgh was reduced to 7 hours 45 minutes, and the return time to London to 7 hours 40 minutes. During the same year, the train crew began to supply newspapers and magazines from WH Smith and John Menzies to passengers and also rented out special headphones at a shilling a time. This was another of Gresley's revolutionary ideas, allowing people to plug a special cable into a socket at the back of their seats and listen to radio and news reports, or enjoy a choice of gramophone music. This service probably introduced Britain's first mobile DJ.

But if the LNER thought it was going to have things all its own way, it had another think coming. An engineering revolution was about to sweep through Europe, and Gresley's talents would be needed more than ever.

At the same time that steam locomotives were being improved by Chapelon's advances in Europe, the advantages of diesel power was also being examined. Eventually diesels would rule the rails, but in Britain experimentation with this new power source was still negligible. In stark contrast, André Chapelon's French railway employers were keen to look at modes of rail transport other than steam, and utilised Chapelon's engineering skills to examine trials on new high-speed diesel electric sets, which were rapidly becoming of interest across Europe.

In 1933, to ensure they kept ahead of the game, the French railway network launched plans for a brand-new test facility at Vitry-sur-Seine, near Paris. This facility was much envied by LNER and other British operators who still dreamed of running their own plant. Gresley attended the opening of the test centre in July, admiring the superb facilities. He believed his own company could soon benefit from tests on his own designs but, in contrast to the French manufacturers, he was instructed to cut back on the development of new steam locomotives. In 1933, his company produced just seventeen engines, compared to thirty-four the previous year.

Gresley, Bulleid and Chapelon, together with several top German engineers including Karl Maybach and Richard Wagner, continued to keep in touch over various developments. Although there was a certain amount of rivalry, each regularly shared updated information and attended international railway congress conferences in Cairo, Madrid and Paris between 1933 and 1936.

To the uninformed, it would appear that the next railway breakthrough would come from France – but the Germans had other ideas. The German railway network had been nationalised in 1920 and four years later the Deutsche Reichsbahn (DR) and the Deutsche Reichsbahn Gesellschaf (DRG) had merged. When the railways had come to Germany in 1835, with an initial service running between Nuremberg and Furth, the locomotive, train and driver were all English. The locomotive, called *Adler* (*Eagle*), was designed by Robert Stephenson in Newcastle. But times had changed.

On 21 June 1931, the German press gave notice to its European rivals of the success of secret testing of high-speed diesel railcars. These new diesels dispensed with a separate locomotive by carrying their engines under the floors of the carriages, thereby increasing operational flexibility and offering great maintenance and construction efficiencies. The report confirmed that an experimental railcar, still under test, had supposedly achieved extremely high speeds.

The German newspaper report highlighted the fact that the new train was 'streamlined', playing on this new addition to the European vocabulary. The German machine was far from conventional, being propelled by a powerful petrol engine and an airscrew propeller arrangement. The operators claimed it had reached the dizzy speed of 143mph, over a distance of more than six miles on a test track between Karstadt and Deginthin on the Berlin to Hamburg line. The news came as a shock to railway designers and engineers across Europe, including Gresley, and started another race, this time to study high-speed diesel-electric sets for possible service in the UK.

This initial German prototype vehicle, called a *Schienenzeppelin*, was the creation of Dr F. Kruckenburg, from the Association for the Advancement of Science, and was not supported by the Reichsbahn. His project ran on the theory of suspending railcars from a motor rail using a diesel engine with hydraulic transmission. Kruckenburg was bitterly disappointed when Reichsbahn officials first rejected his approach, protesting that he had designed it specifically for their use. The company responded by claiming that general interest and marketable value would be limited, and that it preferred to continue with development of their own prototype railcar set, using Maybach engines.

In 1932, undeterred, Kruckenburg returned again to the office of the Reichsbahn chief, Dr Julius Dorpmoller. However, the Reichsbahn was still not interested, arguing that they had not commissioned the idea. Moreover, they believed the propeller could prove dangerous in everyday use – a reasonable enough concern, perhaps. The Reichsbahn also reckoned the construction was too lightweight, had a long wheelbase, and that its air brake was inadequate for high-speed use. Despite several attempts to persuade officials to reconsider, Dorpmoller dismissed Kruckenburg after a brief meeting.

The Reichsbahn already had advanced plans of its own for fast railcars, and for the development of some powerful new steam locomotives. It was involved in the *Einheits* development programme, supervised by Dr Richard Wagner, and had committed a vast budget towards this research. In 1932, DR officials announced (no doubt much to the delight of politicians) that its new *Fliegende Hamburger* train – the famous *Flying Hamburger* – had registered 124mph/198.5kmph on test. There were plans to introduce the trains into public service the following May.

Dr Dorpmoller, then DR's director general, was excited about this new service and thought it could persuade German businessmen to exchange air travel for high-speed train travel, if a guaranteed standard could be maintained. He also declared this new train to be the 'first high-speed inter-city service in the world', a little unfair, perhaps, given that the fastest trains in the UK and the USA at the time were not far off the *Flying Hamburger*'s average speed.

Dorpmoller's latest announcement immediately caught the attention of the British press and the interested public, in particular Nigel Gresley and Oliver Bulleid at King's Cross. Both were well aware of several other key experiments in Germany at that time, in steam and diesel-electric sets, and knew the Reichsbahn and the growing Nazi Party wanted to gain maximum value from any alleged success. At the time breaking air and land speed records was a fanatical obsession, and the two engineers soon set about making provisional arrangements to travel on this new train and to discuss developments with their German counterparts.

Meanwhile, in France, Gresley was beginning to work with the man who would help him develop the design that would lead him to a new world record.

Chapter Six
Streamlined Efficiency

Legendary Italian racing car designer and manufacturer Ettore Bugatti first attracted Nigel Gresley's attention in 1923, when Bugatti's new, streamlined motor designs were unveiled. The two men were probably introduced by W.O. Bentley, who had been a Doncaster railway apprentice under Ivatt, and had also worked with Gresley, later becoming a famous British motor manufacturer. But Bugatti's business association with Gresley only began following a series of misfortunes for Bugatti in the wake of the Wall Street crash.

Bugatti was an impulsive and eccentric man. He dressed casually and preferred bright yellow jumpers, a bowler hat and riding breeches. He was small, with dark, brushed-back hair. He had a thin, delicate face with sharp features, and with his slim physique he might easily have been mistaken for a jockey. The self-trained son of a prominent Italian furniture designer, Carlo Bugatti, he had a reputation for being ostentatious, with expensive sartorial tastes to match.

Bugatti employed over 1200 people at his motor production works at Alsace, and designed an elegant range of motor vehicles not just to look stylish, but to win races. Like Gresley, he worked mainly by trial and error, examining the problems of aerodynamics by strapping huge, wooden shapes to the front of road-test vehicles and measuring the resultant wind resistance. Gresley no doubt became aware of Bugatti's designs because they were light years ahead of their time – and of any rivals – as a result of his use of innovative wind tunnels. But Bugatti used rather primitive road tests to examine and improve the speed and design of his cars, and during one of the first public trials of his latest machines at the famous Tours Grand Prix the cars suddenly became unstable and difficult to steer at high speed. The result was that only one of his cars finished the race and his new cars, though shaped like perfect aerofoils, were unfortunately dubbed 'Tours Tanks'. Critics said they looked like they were 'in danger of taking off' and blamed the new, short body of the car for its uncertain speed and vertical lift problems.

However, Bugatti quickly learned from this humiliation and began to test larger, longer and heavier-bodied vehicles, which had more of a cigar-type shape, aerodynamically designed to keep wind resistance to a minimum. Eventually, this produced his masterpiece, the Type-35. But just as Bugatti was beginning to claw back his fine reputation on the racetrack, he faced more problems due to a fall in demand for his commercial brand vehicle, Master Royale. Bugatti had invested heavily in this grand touring vehicle, weighing more than three tons and some nineteen feet long, which at the time of its production cost more than a Rolls Royce. But now his so-called 'King of Cars' rapidly seemed to be losing its charm, and interest was collapsing as a result of the world recession. By the time of the Wall Street crash in 1929, Bugatti had only sold three cars.

The crash only made things worse and his company produced another three cars before he was forced to admit the failure of the project: he faced bankruptcy. (Ironically, one of these rare and magnificent cars sold in 1987 for £5.5 million at a special auction at London's Royal Albert Hall.) Bugatti was desperate for new business opportunities after being forced to sack more than half his workforce. In order to preserve his reputation and his personal fortune, Bugatti needed a new idea, and fast.

Gresley and his assistant, Oliver Bulleid, had often visited Bugatti in France, and both respected his views on streamlining techniques. They were supporters of his racing car activities and shared his sporting interests. When Bugatti needed advice about a new set of proposals from the French railway operators (who were themselves struggling in the midst of the economic slump), he contacted Gresley and Bulleid at their King's Cross offices to seek their opinion. The French railway, like many other European networks, was still divided into several separate companies, and urgently needed to re-organise itself in the face of fierce competition from other road and air transport operators.

The railways were proposing a programme of redevelopment and were considering the use of new high-speed, lightweight trains. They were facing extreme pressure to switch from established steam to cross-country petrol and diesel railcars. By autumn of that year, Renault, Michelin and many other equally hard-hit French motor product manufacturers had gained lucrative, government-backed contracts to design and develop the production of these new railway sets. Bugatti, too, wanted to become involved but his health had suffered, mainly from the stress and strain following the stockmarket crash. However, throughout that winter he worked on – from home, and mainly from his bed, dressed in pyjamas and a dressing gown. He worked around the clock to produce some incredibly detailed and highly imaginative sketches for the French railcars of the future.

Bugatti's designs were extraordinary, with smoothly rounded corners and innovative wedge-shaped front and rear ends. They were roughly based on his earlier 'Tours Tanks' ideas, but the carriage designs were both long and heavy enough to avoid the previous instability. He used four in-line petrol engines, which were again similar in design and appearance to his old Royal car engines. Bugatti built a prototype at his factory in the spring of 1933 – before he had even had time to construct a railway track and sidings. This rush job provided its own peculiar problems, and when it finally became time to transport his construction, half the town turned out to see it carefully manoeuvred through the narrow streets and along twisting roads from the factory to the railway yards.

The model proved a great success in trials and more than satisfied the railway management. Within months, Bugatti railcars began to run in full service between Paris and Deauville, often reaching 113mph/180kph during high-speed rail tests. Bugatti's prototype constructions seemed faster than rival Reichsbahn railcars that were still undergoing secret tests, but he remained hampered by onerous French rail safety restrictions. This meant that several new prototype railcars in Germany, running between Berlin and Hamburg, took the plaudits, eventually securing a record speed of 122mph/196kph.

Within a short period, however, Bugatti had seventy-six railcars of various types and designs running on railway networks throughout France. All ran at much greater average speeds than steam locos, although most were much more uncomfortable until after the war. They were also heavy on fuel, often using more than a litre per kilometre, which guaranteed they would not survive long after the war.

Bugatti's modified aerodynamic designs helped create a more efficient type of high-speed railcar, and interest soon spread throughout Europe and, eventually, to America. Competition from other forms of transport, including motorcars and aircraft, stimulated interest in this research and encouraged worldwide competition. Gresley remained fascinated by these developments and began to incorporate these new streamlining ideas into his own steam locomotive designs. The LNER were keen to make existing railway timetables faster to attract the public back onto the trains, and in both France and Britain there was a need for new and updated rolling stock, and powerful, streamlined engines for heavy-haul duties. Gresley once again set his mind to the job.

From the early 1930s onwards, Gresley experimented with various ideas for streamlining steam locomotives. He remained concerned about the perennial problem of smoke constantly obscuring a driver's view. Moreover, the driver was working from a small observation window, which meant that high-speed steam working could be dangerous without a guaranteed clear vision of the track and signals ahead. Bugatti recognised there was an urgent need to rectify this problem and began using a horizontal wedge at the front end to lift the smoke over the top of the loco. He also examined other experimental designs, some dating back to the 1880s from the United States and Germany, which favoured a more vertical wedge, pushing the air flow along both sides of the engine, though Bugatti found the horizontal wedge more successful.

Gresley was delighted, saying this design not only helped lift smoke clear on most occasions but also reduced wind resistance and avoided disturbance to other passing trains. Bugatti's successful new shapes gave locomotives a somewhat bull-nosed, thrusting appearance, which was often preferred in America. Gresley tested these designs at the City and Guilds Engineering College in London and the National Railway Physical Laboratory (NPL) at Teddington, and found them more reliable than their predecessors.

Gresley involved his friend and former colleague, Professor W.E. Dalby, and the eminent scientist F.C. Johansen of the NPL in these tests as well. The professor, who had formerly held an engineering apprenticeship at Stratford works under the former Great Eastern Railway banner, worked at the City and Guilds College in London and later established an engineering department at LNER chief general manager Wedgwood's former university, Cambridge. He offered Gresley some independent advice and the CME made extensive use of his valuable knowledge and research in later years. Johansen had presented a paper to the Institution of Locomotive Engineers about wind-tunnel testing in relation to streamlining effects for locomotives and rolling stock, and offered a personal interpretation based on tests at the NPL. About the same time, other railway organisations, including the

LMS, LNER and SR, commissioned the NPL to examine wind-resistance methods. In 1932 Johansen left the NPL to establish his own research facility in Derby.

Gresley and Bulleid later travelled on one of Bugatti's railcars, in the company of the Italian designer, for a comparative test with the *Flying Hamburger*. Gresley found Bugatti an 'animated and impetuous host'. Both LNER men journeyed between Paris and Le Havre, and Paris and Deauville in 1933, and were thrilled by the striking wedge-shaped front end of the train. However, not all went according to plan, and both later admitted they had had a 'hair-raising ride' in one of the new railcars as it travelled at more than 80mph towards the centre of Paris. Gresley reported that it rode 'very badly' and was 'bumpy' and claimed he had to sit on top of the petrol tank. When the CME asked what would happen in the event of a fire, Bugatti answered blithely, 'There could be a fire, but it would be a hundred yards behind the vehicle before it broke out'; a response that Gresley did not find entirely reassuring.

Bulleid shared Bugatti's scepticism about using small-scale wooden models in wind tunnels and agreed it would be better to see full-size models in action as tested on road vehicles, but with a locomotive this proved near impossible. The LNER engineers were always trying to improve their designs, but were not totally convinced by Bugatti's wind-flow experiments. They spoke at length with Dr Richard Wagner at the German Reichsbahn, who came to a similar assessment. The plan, however, wasn't necessarily to use these new designs for railcars, but to get the very most possible out of the LNER's steam locomotives.

On 30 January 1933, events in Germany dominated the newspapers of the world. The country's ageing president, Paul von Hindenburg, summoned Adolf Hitler to his office and confirmed his appointment as the new Chancellor of the Third Reich. He would soon be Führer of all Germany.

Hitler's main aims on gaining power included reducing unemployment, increasing Germany's industrial capabilities and creating showpiece projects for the rest of the world to admire. Pumping funds into the railway system achieved all three. In later years, experts claimed that in fact the Reichsbahn had provided the bulk of the finance from their own resources, but the new German government was naturally keen to take the glory for high-speed railcar development, and used its success for propaganda purposes. The propaganda minister, Goebbels, soon announced plans to build a first railway tunnel under Berlin, calling for the design of new modern railway stations. He boasted that the development of Germany's rail network would be a 'demonstration of national capabilities' and asked fellow ministers to call the country's top railway officials to a special meeting. The architect Albert Speer, another key member of Hitler's team, was also involved in the development of the Autobahn and Reichsbahn rail network, overseeing the work of Richard Brademann, who designed the new stations. As Hitler hoped, the programme soon helped reduce unemployment, providing new opportunities for many Germans and a sense of prosperity and achievement throughout the country.

Throughout 1933, Germany's railways underwent a massive but necessary overhaul as Hitler and his Nazi colleagues planned to put the Reichsbahn back on track. Dorpmoller, the head of the Deutsche Reichsbahn (and later Hitler's Minister of Transport), became temporary co-ordinator of the new developments; Dr Richard Wagner and several others also contributed ideas. The ambitious new project was regarded as a unique opportunity for the new 'friends of the Reich'. Backed by thousands of Brownshirts, or Storm Troopers as they became known, Hitler now had a vast army of helpers to ensure his orders were obeyed.

The *Flying Hamburger* itself was exactly the sort of propaganda Goebbels and the Third Reich revelled in, and they promoted it enthusiastically, Goebbels describing the service as 'the fastest train in the world'. It was successful from the beginning and the Deutsche Reichsbahn soon ordered several further sets for construction, intended for routes from Berlin to Cologne, Frankfurt, Nuremberg, Munich and Stuttgart.

In Britain, Gresley and his colleagues wondered whether there was anything they could learn from Germany's extraordinary redevelopment programme. Moreover, they wondered if they would be able to compete on the European stage in the future, given the substantial amount of government investment in the German rail system. The CME was intrigued but also alarmed by these sudden developments. Although Gresley was not a politician, he was well versed in current affairs and was worried about Hitler's growing stranglehold on Germany. He shared the concern of many at the news of constant threats and intimidation to minority groups, together with the steady build-up of military operations. He continued to retain a friendship with the senior politician in waiting, Winston Churchill, and no doubt discussed current events with him.

Gresley warned Bulleid to be careful and awaited confirmation from his German engineering colleagues that his proposal to travel on the *Flying Hamburger* would be accepted and welcomed. Gresley may well have hoped that Germany's outspoken new Chancellor would fall flat on his face in the attempt to re-build and revive the railways. He remained optimistic and ambitious, however, about his own steam developments and was keen to return to France and discuss matters again with both Chapelon and Bugatti. He clearly valued their opinions and was curious about a number of other alleged secret German tests.

Gresley, Bulleid, Wedgwood and the LNER board met in May 1933 to decide whether to investigate the Third Reich's boastful claim of high-speed diesel-electric rail sets. Bolstered both by the magnificent non-stop running of the *Flying Scotsman*, and by

Gresley's determination to construct a new breed of powerful Pacifics, the team agreed to check out the Reichsbahn claims first hand. If the results proved satisfactory, the LNER board would consider testing the train in Britain.

Gresley had obviously read trade and public press reports about Dr Kruckenberg's unorthodox *Schienenzeppelin* and watched with interest as the *Flying Hamburger*, VT-877, was first tested. Its first run in 1932 had claimed a speed of 124mph/198.5 kmph and the train came into public service on 15 May 1933. It was scheduled to cover a distance of 178 miles between Berlin and Hamburg at an average speed of 77.4mph. Reichsbahn chief Dr Julius Dorpmoller, by now one of Hitler's rising industrial stars, made a propaganda broadcast boasting of the speed the two-car articulated unit could attain, and explaining that the train was particularly aimed at the lucrative business market.

It was a handsome as well as efficient package. Tested in secret 'Zeppelin' wind tunnels at a special test plant using reduced-scale models, it had special designer-rounded corners at the top of the body and ends that curved sharply downwards, with sheet metal reaching down to the rails. It had a lightweight frame and the motor fitted under the floor, and the train headlights resembled huge bulging eyes. The driving wheels were connected to an electrical circuit and powered by two Maybach Motor Works engines each of 410hp; Maybach had worked on a series of experiments for about three years before perfecting this particular design. The train also used a new type of automatic signalling and braking system necessary for the high speeds. The designers had tried to perfect modern safety measures and operated a revolutionary electro-magnetic train control system. The Germans tested this method extensively, claiming no parts of the power plant made contact with the rails and boasting that some 1600 miles of network was equipped with this inductive signalling and safety sys tem. If a train exceeded the required limit or raced past a signal, a warning bell would sound and the automatic braking system would immediately bring the service to a halt.

The coaches were built in two halves with two axles at either end and a common axle in the centre; it was a design influenced by Gresley, who had developed articulated coaches, with a wheelset between two linked coaches. There were no separate compartments and each half formed one large saloon, with luggage stored in the forward baggage department. Passengers had a waiter service with warm and cold drinks, but only cold buffet-style food. There was also a bar in the centre of the train. The units originally appeared with bogies painted in black and skirts in aluminium, and had ivory bands above the windows, with a violet band beneath; these were later amended to two black bands and two ivory bands (with occasional variations). Although most of the other Reichsbahn trains did not receive Nazi regalia until a year or so later, the Germans were so proud of this particular service that many of the *Hamburger* trains soon started to display distinctive swastika emblems. By 1934, the new Nazi government had taken control of all rail operations, and Hitler ordered all steam locomotives, diesel sets and rolling stock to use Nazi swastikas and the German Eagle. Platforms and stations also carried similar flags and Party decorations.

In order to advance the high-speed development, the Reichsbahn tried to compete with motor coaches over shorter distances. It became almost obsessed with saving time and money, and considered 100mph as a suitable working speed. To accommodate some additional fast working, the Reichsbahn sometimes had to readjust the track layout, reducing curves.

Initially the *Flying Hamburger* carried 102 passengers, soon increased to 140, reached a maximum speed of 100mph, and recorded an average speed of 77.4mph from Berlin to Hamburg, and 76.3mph in the reverse direction on a 178.1-mile journey. Its regular performances impressed engineers worldwide. Timetables indicated an average running speed of 80mph and, by 1935, the Germans claimed they would soon offer twelve of the fastest railway journeys in the world, with average speeds ranging from 75 to 83mph. The service from Cologne to Berlin, a total distance of 359 miles with six stops, took some 5 hours 10 minutes outward, and 4 hours 57 minutes on the return leg. The Cologne to Hamburg service was a journey of some 280 miles, achieved in 4 hours 18 minutes northbound, and 4 hours 6 minutes southbound, including seven stops.

The *Flying Hamburger* train soon became famous throughout the world. Its popularity was such that seats had to be booked many weeks before. The German public called it a 'Zeppelin on rails' and, using Bugatti's concepts, it was streamlined for speed. The sets compared favourably with Bugatti's rival French railcars but, not surprisingly, the Germans claimed their units were faster and technically more efficient. Goebbels continually boasted about the capabilities of the *Flying Hamburger*, though other foreign experts and visitors disagreed, and some complained of cramped conditions and a constant rolling motion.

At the time, Deutsche Reichsbahn was one of the few railway networks that served the whole of its country. Goebbels' publicity department claimed that 700,000 people worked for the organisation by the mid-1930s and that there was no other similar network in the world. It boasted that by comparison with France and Britain, the Germans were 'vastly superior, better organised and more efficient'. This was a claim that Gresley reluctantly agreed with and that prompted him to revise his own plans as soon as possible.

The French, however, were restricted by track speed safety regulations, which allowed speeds up to a maximum of 87mph on suitable lines. By then Bugatti was running twice-daily services from Paris to Havre on the main line, a distance of 141.5 miles, in two hours, registering an average speed of 70.8mph including stops. The quickest reported time was from Havre to Rouen, a distance of 54.9 miles with a steep gradient, completed in just forty-five minutes. The Frenchman's units were also in regular use on other popular routes, especially in the summer season at Etat, and a twice-daily service to the seaside resort of Trouville-Deauville, which again included a long gradient. Throughout Europe, there was similar development of high-speed diesel-electric services but France and Germany led the way.

It was only a month or so after the official launch of the *Flying Hamburger* service in May 1933 that LNER officials first travelled to Berlin to experience life on the extraordinary train. Oliver Bulleid made the first official contact, with a brief from Gresley. The Germans, naturally keen to promote their new services, seemed delighted to arrange a meeting with Reichsbahn officials and visiting rail engineers. Visas and applications to travel on the train were quickly endorsed.

Bulleid travelled with a small party of LNER staff from London. On arrival, their German hosts made them very welcome. Reports said the UK contingent were well received and, according to Bulleid, they were given 'hearty meals and a comfortable journey' on the round trip from Berlin to Hamburg. Bulleid noted that, compared to the busy East Coast line, the line had limited traffic. He was slightly annoyed that the Germans were reluctant to discuss any technical matters. They also refuted allegations of any running or mechanical problems and denied the group access to watch servicing or maintenance. After discussion, Bulleid could see no point in his group remaining in Germany and reluctantly sent them back home. He himself, however, stayed on for a few days, determined to get some genuine answers from the man responsible for the development of the train.

Aware of the growing tensions throughout Germany and the recent violence in Berlin (not to mention the almost overpowering presence of Brownshirts and the Gestapo), Bulleid quickly made his way via a series of inter-city trains to Munich for a special meeting with Dr Maybach. It seems a brave decision given the circumstances, since Bulleid could well have been considered an industrial spy. Fortunately, their discussions proved beneficial and Bulleid learned much about the performance and development of the *Flying Hamburger*. After all, Maybach, Bulleid and Gresley were old friends and, despite restrictions, had often met and discussed new developments. All three were genuine railway engineers rather than political puppets.

Bulleid found that, contrary to Third Reich propaganda, the train had suffered numerous problems during tests. These problems had been highlighted during trials in Holland, when the instructions of the manufacturers had not been followed to their full extent. However, the train's speed and the adaptations to rolling stock remained impressive. The LNER board told Gresley that they had been impressed with the overall performances of the *Flying Hamburger* and asked him if he thought it would be capable of maintaining a tight schedule on the East Coast route; they wanted to explore the possibility of similar rail trials in England. It was a remarkable example of the open-mindedness the LNER had when it came to improving its services.

In 1934, Gresley personally examined the service himself, writing in a subsequent report:

> I visited Germany in the latter part of 1934 and travelled on the *Flying Hamburger* from Berlin to Hamburg. I was so much impressed with the smooth running of this train at a speed of 100mph, which was maintained for long distances, that I thought it advisable to explore the possibilities of extra high-speed travel for experimental purposes on the LNER.
>
> With a thoroughness characteristic of the German engineers, they made a very exhaustive investigation and prepared a complete schedule showing the shortest possible running times under favourable conditions. They then added ten per cent, which they regarded as adequate to meet varying weather conditions and to have sufficient time in reverse to make up for such decelerations or delays as might normally be expected.

The train, weighing 115 tons, was to consist of three articulated coaches and to be generally similar to the German train. The times for the complete journey were given as 4 hours 15 minutes in the down. The train provided seating for 140 passengers.

So far, so good, but the accommodation was much more cramped than that provided in this country for ordinary third-class passengers, and it did not appear likely to prove attractive for a journey occupying 4 hours.

LNER staff had given the German engineers all the particulars of the East Coast Main Line: Gresley was interested to see what they could achieve. Like Wedgwood, Gresley still believed his steam locomotives could do better, arguing that they would also be able to haul much heavier loads in comfort, and with proper refreshment facilities.

Nonetheless, Gresley was impressed by the service. He contacted Maybach again and asked him to prepare a detailed estimate for the Board, based on a three-car set working between King's Cross and Newcastle for a four-hour schedule. Gresley sent the Germans an extensive pack of information, which included track data and gradients, curves and weather conditions. He even sent information concerning maintenance requirements, together with passenger details.

Chapter Seven
Faster and Faster

The French and Germans were not the LNER's only rivals. Closer to home, an engineering revolution was about to sweep through the LMS following the appointment of an exciting new chief engineer.

Born the same year as Gresley, on 27 May 1876, William Stanier was educated at Wycliffe College, in Gloucestershire. His father worked for the Great Western Railway and, as in so many railway families, it seemed only natural that young William should follow in his father's footsteps. He first started as an apprentice to William Dean, spending the first five years learning his trade. During the First World War, Stanier was responsible for re-tooling of munitions at Swindon works, and two years later he became works manager, then assistant, to Charles Collett, GWR's post-war chief mechanical engineer. Stanier worked closely with Collett at GWR, helping with designs and the development of the famous Castle and King classes. The latter was an expanded Castle which GWR claimed was the most powerful locomotive in the country at the time.

Following the 1923 grouping, the LMS inherited a variety of locomotive works at Crewe, Derby and Horwich. Like the LNER, the company found itself with many underpowered and outdated engines and poor-quality rolling stock. In 1926, Sir Josiah Stamp was recruited to supervise a complete revamp of the company. Acting in the manner of an American-style executive, Stamp faced the difficult task of reorganisation – made worse in the middle of the recession – and quickly replaced the company's general managers and its main committee. Within the year he was elected chairman. Like Wedgwood at the LNER,

Stamp wanted to create unity and harmony between the various companies and in order to do so he needed to standardise operating methods and equipment. He gave his then CME, Sir Henry Fowler, a target to produce more powerful steam locomotives but he was also keen to reduce maintenance and operating costs by the elimination of double-heading on major high-speed passenger expresses.

In 1932, Sir Henry Fowler retired, and Stanier moved from the GWR at Swindon to become chief mechanical engineer with the LMS based at Euston station. Like Gresley, he was one of the top railway engineers in the country. But despite their professional rivalry, Stanier and Gresley had a very strong personal friendship and a close working relationship which continued for decades. Gresley's daughter, Vi, was also a friend of Stanier's daughter, Joan. Stanier's son was a friend of Geoffrey Godfrey, another engineer, to whom he had introduced Vi; the couple later married. In later years, Vi and Geoffrey were often visitors at the Staniers' home.

Stanier was a competent engineer and a first-class organiser, who, like Gresley when he was first appointed CME, faced an immense task: his brief was to commence an extensive, if not dramatic, rebuilding programme on a limited budget. He had inherited one of the largest transport organisations in the world and was responsible for 6870 route miles of railway. The LMS then had massive commercial interests in Europe, including a hotel chain, plus a host of administrative problems. In particular, Stanier identified a desperate shortage of heavy express and freight locomotives. He was instructed to upgrade motive power as soon as possible in order to meet increasing demands, and formulated a five-year plan of restructuring. His new office was less than a mile from Gresley's at King's Cross and the two men often met to discuss matters. Stanier, too, had a reputation as a tough taskmaster and regularly investigated failures in service. With his vast engineering experience he could soon spot boiler, brake and mechanical faults and tried to learn from his mistakes. He was generally considered a kindly man able to converse with staff at all levels. Stanier was particularly interested in the potential for steam-turbine motive power and, like Gresley, he was a keen traveller and investigator, who once visited Sweden and India to examine new developments.

Between 1932 and 1948, Stanier oversaw the building of some 2000 locomotives, containing many features and modifications from his former GWR days, including adaptations to valve gear and boiler designs. He also organised a vast modernisation plan to deal with carriage design and workshops, introduced standard-isation, and ultimately saved the LMS more than two million pounds through reduced repair and operating costs.

Stanier soon improved mass-production techniques and began designing new corridor carriages, improving both comfort and speed and eventually providing the necessary motive power required. During this period he also created some of the most notable locomotives in LMS history, including the Black 5 for mixed traffic: some 800 of this rugged workmanlike engine were built, and could be seen operating from Inverness to Bournemouth. He also built the famous and popular Jubilee class locomotives.

During 1933, Stanier introduced his first LMS Pacific, No. 6200, *Princess Royal*. Broadly speaking, this was a rival to Gres-ley's A1 class, already publicly acclaimed, and the new locomo-tive soon became a great source of rivalry to the LNER. Its sister engine, No. 6201, *Princess Elizabeth*, later travelled from London to Glasgow in just 5 hours 44 minutes, recording an average speed of 70mph. Further development of this design would later create the famed Princess Coronation class – a giant of a design which eventually produced the greatest recorded cylinder power of any steam locomotive in this country. It would not just be a rival to the A3 – it would pose a stiff challenge for Gresley to improve on it.

Not a man who liked to be outdone, Stanier took advantage of renewed interest in rail speed publicity to make his own mark through a series of new brake tests (commonly known as speed trials) and developments of his LMS Pacific locomotives. He began with a remarkable series of trials on 19 and 20 September 1933. A Midlands motor company had chartered some special LMS trains, and this gave Stanier a perfect opportunity to test high-speed running. He used the LMS new three-cylinder 4-6-0 Royal Scot class, *Comet*. The engine gave a powerful performance, running from Coventry on the 'up' journey to a signal by Euston station, a distance of 93.5 miles, in just 74 minutes and 20 seconds, inclusive of several delays. On four occasions, the engine exceeded 90mph, the maximum being 92mph. Over the two days, this locomotive made four round trips with an average load of 275 tons and covered 235 miles at an overall average speed of 79.1mph.

The trials sounded as an alarm to Gresley and colleagues at LNER, who began to closely monitor other potential rival attempts. If they were to retain their British crown they could not afford to take their eye off the ball.

Stanier was back in action again the following year, with another trial on 6 April 1934. The *Princess Royal* hauled the 5.25 p.m. express from Liverpool to London Euston, completing the journey in 134 minutes and 37 seconds. It maintained an average speed of 70.5mph and did not exceed 85mph – a marvellous demonstration of the power of his new designs. The LMS chief was delighted by the results, especially with such a heavy twelve-coach train of 380 tons – and allowing for unfortunate slowings at Stafford and Rugby.

However, despite substantial progress on many speed fronts, Stanier and his LMS colleagues gained a reputation for ignoring the problems of secondary or small branch lines. Local trains were often said to be slow and dirty compared to mainline services, with management adopting a policy of strict economy so that stations were rarely maintained or even painted. This was in stark contrast to the LNER, who always boasted about the appearance and efficiency of all their outlets and staff.

Critics, too, often attacked Stanier's lack of construction at major terminals – Leeds City was the only station to be rebuilt – claiming LMS operations paled into insignificance compared to those of their rival the LNER. The two companies went head to head in marketing, with the LMS often using the LNER idea of pictorial colour posters to promote its own holidays. The LMS, too, commissioned many new top artists, and in addition made considerable use of promotional films and railway propaganda.

As the depression continued throughout Britain and most parts of Europe, Cecil Dandridge, the LNER marketing chief, faced considerable pressure from the board to cut costs. He looked at the numbers and types of promotional posters produced and decided that the seaside locations and other tourist spots could probably contribute the most towards the cost of marketing and production. So he created more than forty brilliant pictorial posters promoting seaside towns on the East Coast and Scotland. He later claimed to have commissioned more than a thousand designs over the course of his career; fortunately, for the future of his department, he persuaded tourist town authorities to share expenses.

Poster designs kept pace with rapid rail developments. Gresley's Pacifics provided many new marketing opportunities and, together with the development of other new express trains, the LNER's range of catchy new slogans began to make an impression on the public. Many appeared in newspapers and on station promotions, including *It's Quicker by Rail; Scotland for the Highlands; Shortest and Quickest – East Coast for Comfort; Harwich for the Continent; King's Cross for Scotland – East Coast Route; Meet the Sun on the East Coast* and *York – on the Route of the Flying Scotsman*. Seventy years on, they haven't dated: the simplicity of their message is their brilliance.

The artist Tom Purvis produced a memorable poster in the late 1930s with a design of four of Gresley's new Pacifics, and Frank Mason, who was a superb marine artist, created a brilliant design advertising Harwich sailings and those of the ocean liner *Queen Mary* (and later *Queen Elizabeth*). Mason's colleague Frank Newbould produced *Britain's Fast Streamlined Train,* and the rest of the art team designed many other colourful covers for walking holidays, railway handbooks and weekend cruises.

Dandridge was keen on improving LNER morale and wanted minor stations and staff to feel part of the network. He took on board suggestions from the company chairman, William Whitelaw, and endorsed competitions for the best-kept station in different categories. He also promoted garden displays, which he later claimed to be among the finest in the country. The company also began to make use of radio promotions, capitalising on the Post Office's famous 1936 publicity film *Night Mail*, with words by W.H. Auden and music by Benjamin Britten (*'This is the night mail crossing the border / Bringing the cheque and the postal order / Letters for the rich, letters for the poor / The shop at the corner, the girl next door'*). The film became enormously popular, and both adults and children often sang along when it was shown at local cinemas.

At last, Gresley received confirmation of test proposals on the East Coast line from Maybach and his German engineering colleagues. Despite all the hype that surrounded the *Flying Hamburger*, the results were disappointing. With restrictions, the Germans could not promise better than four and a half hours for the 268-mile journey from King's Cross to Newcastle and were, as expected, unable to offer any hot meals to passengers. Moreover, the LNER board had rigid standards and thought that the diesel sets did not match the company image portrayed by the marketing and publicity department. They believed their customers expected a high standard of service and seemed more disturbed by the idea of the cold buffet offered on the German train than any failure to meet other criteria. Once again then, the stage was set for Gresley, who still firmly believed he could do much better with steam. He decided to try to prove the point. Wedgwood shared Gresley's belief that steam had a future and supported his proposal for additional experiments and future brake trials using established Pacific locomotives.

The views of the LNER board were not unanimous. In the autumn of 1934, none other than the LNER company chairman himself, William Whitelaw, told a meeting at the Institute of Transport that his East Coast network was 'unsuited for high-speed running', telling members it was 'honeycombed with underground workings'. He was speaking nothing but the truth: the East Coast Main Line passed (and still passes) over the once great coalfields of Yorkshire, Nottinghamshire and East Scotland. When underground workings collapse, they cause the ground above to subside and become uneven – hardly conducive to safe high-speed running. The problem still exists today: millions of pounds were recently spent on rerouting the same main line at Dolphingstone, near Prestonpans, to avoid precisely the same problems that Whitelaw discussed in 1934.

But this was not to stop the LNER's greatest triumph yet. On 30 November 1934, Gresley's high-speed theories were finally put to the test. After weeks of preparation and planning with his colleagues, he instructed one of his top drivers, the legendary Bill Sparshatt, to 'run as hard as he liked' with A1 class, No. 4472, *Flying Scotsman*, on a regulated test run between King's Cross and Leeds Central. It was a distance of just over 185 miles on a provisional schedule of 165 minutes each way, allowing for an average speed of 67.6mph. The fastest time achieved to date had been 193 minutes.

On the northbound leg, the engine hauled just four coaches weighing a total of 145 tons to Leeds in 152 minutes. On the return trip two additional coaches were added, making a revised load of 295 tons. Fortune certainly favoured the brave and the train made the return journey in a new Leeds to London record time of 157 minutes and 15 seconds – registering a magnificent 100mph on the descent from Stoke Tunnel, between Grantham and Peterborough near Little Bytham. Oliver Bulleid was on the footplate as No. 4472 achieved the 100mph record and confirmed the train included the dynamometer car, a restaurant car and two standard coaches. The speed never dipped below 81mph with a maximum of 95mph on the journey to Leeds, and reached 100mph on the 'up' leg to King's Cross. His report confirmed the train weight was more than 30 tons heavier than the German diesel car proposal and he was thrilled by the outstanding performance, which he agreed encouraged further experimentation.

This incredible return performance by the eleven-year-old engine, achieved despite severe slowing over various junctions, also registered 40 miles at an average of 90mph, and, for a distance of 600 yards on the southbound journey, 100mph. *City of Truro* had achieved a similar speed in 1904 but her record had never been authenticated. This was the first time a dynamometer car had travelled at more than 100mph and the result set a new British rail speed record, into the bargain helping provide the CME with further evidence of the capacity of high-speed steam.

Cecil J. Allen, in his capacity as train reporter, was an important witness on both the *Flying Scotsman* brake tests in November 1934 and then with *Papyrus* in March 1935. He publicised *Flying Scotsman*'s achievement of the magic hundred, and also wrote about Gresley's consideration of the *Hamburger* plan and the LNER proposals for high-speed steam running.

Still determined to push his theory to the limit, Gresley made additional preparations for another brake trial to be held in the spring of 1935, believing that another promising performance would finally convince the board of the need for his more updated Pacifics. The trial was a success but Gresley didn't want to build more of his existing designs, writing later: 'I felt that to secure a sufficient margin of power it would be essential to streamline the engine and train as effectively as possible, and at the same time to make sundry alterations to the design of the cylinders and boiler which would conduce to freer running and to secure an ample reverse of power for fast uphill running.'

With his firm belief that steam could rule the day, combined with the ongoing competition from his rival Stanier at LMS, Gresley had set himself an enormous challenge. He still wanted to prove his point, believing strongly in 'horses for courses', but needed to supply his board with positive proof that a new breed of Pacific was necessary to keep pace with other British and European locomotives. So Gresley set about a series of important tasks. First he secured an order from the board to develop a new P2 class 2-8-2, locomotive No. 2001, *Cock o' the North*. This engine would be his guinea pig and he would continually modify the design to include the very latest improvements. He was pre-pared to see it as an experimental model rather than a template for series production in order to extend and improve his knowl-edge of heavy-duty working.

The P2 was designed for long-haul passenger services and to eliminate double-heading on the tough route from Edinburgh to Aberdeen. This line offered a serious challenge to any engine, consisting as it did of heavy gradients with sharp curves. At the time of construction, *Cock o' the North* was the most powerful express locomotive in Britain. It had huge driving wheels and was another of Gresley's impressive three-cylinder engines. This exceptional development incorporated four pairs of coupled driving wheels instead of three and was a revolutionary design, including the theoretically more efficient and controllable poppet valve gear. Bugatti's extraordinary wedge-shaped front end gave the locomotive an ultra-modern appearance, radically different from anything else in Britain at the time.

The locomotive hauled passenger expresses of more than 550 tons but tests suggested its performance was likely to be restricted due to a long and rigid wheelbase. Running costs, too, began to increase as it obviously demanded high maintenance. Once again, influenced by Chapelon, Gresley added many more modifications to his test designs. Some of these included ideas to help reduce the loss of steam pressure between the regulator and high-pressure cylinders, while others involved experiments with Lentz poppet valves so that they could open and shut much more quickly without throttling the steam.

Cock o' the North already incorporated many proven additions to established modifications but Gresley later added smoke deflectors following wind tunnel tests at the French plant and in England. The locomotive ran well on initial trials in early 1934, running from King's Cross to Yorkshire and making an immediate visual impact on the public. It ran up Stoke summit with a 650-ton load, consisting of nineteen coaches plus the dynamometer car, at an average speed of nearly 60mph.

In December 1934, less than a month after the successful performance of *Flying Scotsman*, Gresley decided to take up an offer from Chapelon to test *Cock o' the North* with extensive trials in France, his aim being to push the engine to the limit at Chapelon's test plant under Bulleid's supervision. He hoped this might provide the final pieces to the jigsaw in which he sought perfection. Just before Christmas, he sent Oliver Bulleid to France, together with both the locomotive and some of his own rolling stock. Bulleid remained throughout most of the testing and Gresley made infrequent visits. In the same month, Gresley read test reports on the production of a second P2 engine, *Earl Marischal*. It had left Doncaster in October to begin trials and was very similar to No. 2001, with additional modifications to valve running gear (two years later, Gresley added two more upgraded engines to the class and, once again, all were streamlined with Bugatti-style front ends).

Cock o' the North pulled a train of some ten wagons to Harwich, packed with the coal she would use in her tests, while Bulleid travelled across on the Channel ferry. On arrival on the continent, the locomotive ran from Zeebrugge in Belgium to Chapelon's plant near Paris. *Cock o' the North* arrived in excellent working order and began a planned three weeks of extensive trials. Bulleid found the French engineers extremely helpful and cooperative, especially when the engine developed problems with a hot axlebox. Keeping axleboxes cool is vital for the smooth running of a locomotive. If the lubrication fails and they get too hot, the wheels will seize, wrecking the wheels and valve motion.

Bulleid agreed to take the engine to an electric testing centre where the main driving wheels were removed and examined at another location. He arranged for special transportation by lorry across the outskirts of Paris. This journey stimulated tremendous interest amongst the French public and achieved unexpected national publicity. The work was completed overnight and the wheels returned so that the engine was ready for action again the following morning. Unfortunately, the checks failed to eliminate the problem and the engine was removed to another centre at Tours. But the problems were finally fixed, and engineers put the locomotive to work on a series of new tests between Tours and Orleans.

The locomotive was also checked with one of their dynamometer cars, and hauled three four-cylinder French engines that were not in steam. The French test inspector said the engine ran well but claimed the fireman was 'hard pressed' and said that he was 'concerned' by the number of shovel loads of coal needed. The LNER's shovels were only about half the size of the French equivalent, and of a slightly different and narrower shape, due to the smaller coal hole in the firebox. French examiners predicted that the locomotive could never develop the power required.

More tests were then undertaken at Vitry, where engineers again noted that both the axleboxes and axles were running hot. They found that the sacrificial white metal used to line the axle

Sir Nigel Gresley on the locomotive footplate at King's Cross on 15 June 1937, with the Canadian High Commissioner, the Hon. Vincent Massey, for the naming ceremony of No 4489 *Dominion of Canada*. *Picture courtesy of Gresley Society Trust*

Oliver Bulleid was Gresley's long serving loyal deputy, who played a key role in the LNER's success story before eventually joining the Southern Railway as chief mechanical engineer. *Milepost 92 ¹/₂*

Nigel Gresley with his son Roger at his home in Hadley Wood about 1925. *Geoffrey Hughes collection - courtesy of Gresley Society Trust*

P2 Class No. 2001, *Cock o' the North*, as originally built in 1935 with Lentz poppet valve gear. *Geoffrey Hughes collection – courtesy of Gresley Society Trust*

Nigel Gresley on the platform at an official inspection of his new experimental locomotive, the 'Hush-Hush' 4-6-4 No. 10000. He is pictured with Marjorie and Vi Gresley. *Geoffrey Hughes collection – courtesy of Gresley Society Trust*

One of Ettore Bugatti's famous streamlined sports cars at the Paris Motor Show in 1936. *Corbis*

The world-famous diesel railcar the 'Flying Hamburger', which registered 124mph in tests, much to the delight of German Reichsbahn officials. *Milepost 92 ½*

A1 Pacific No. 4472 *Flying Scotsman* – one of Gresley's most famous locomotives and another record breaker and popular crowd pleaser. *British Rail*

Nigel Gresley seen feeding his beloved Mallard ducks at Salisbury Hall around 1934. *Geoffrey Hughes collection*

Sir William Stanier – a good friend of Gresley's, despite being the chief mechanical engineer of his arch rivals LMS. *Milepost 92 ¹/₂*

Sir William Stanier's record-breaking rival locomotive No. 6220 *Coronation* – claimed to be the fastest in the world at the time. *Milepost 92 ¹/₂*

Streamlined No. 2512 *Silver Fox*, seen here in its original silver livery, was the last of the initial batch of four A4 class locomotives, and proved another winner for Gresley.

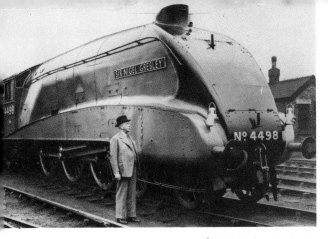

Sir Nigel Gresley beside No. 4498, the A4 Pacific locomotive named after him.

A4 class No. 4498 *Sir Nigel Gresley* approaching Potters Bar with a down Coronation Express. *Geoffrey Hughes – Gresley Society Trust*

Inside the superbly designed Dynamometer car. The photograph confirms the coach had a decorative ceramic patterned toilet and washbasin. *Don Hale*

The famous Dynamometer car used with *Mallard* to confirm her speed on the record run is still coupled to her in the National Railway Museum at York. The North Eastern Railway built the beautiful luxurious testing coach No. 902502 in 1906. *Don Hale*

Some of the dazzling glass and brass instruments can still be seen inside the Dynamometer coach at York Museum. *Don Hale*

A4 class No. 4468 *Mallard* at Barkston just before commencing its record-breaking run on 3 July 1938. *H.M. Hoather – Gresley Society Trust*

A4 class No. 4468 *Mallard* at Peterborough station after reaching 126mph. Pictured are (left) fireman Tommy Bray with driver Joe Duddington and inspector Sam Jenkins. H.M. Hoather – Gresley Society Trust

Confirmation of the World Steam Record – the article in the London *Times* from the following day, Monday 4 July 1938.

Former LNER No. 4468, now BR No. 60022 *Mallard* shown at King's Cross station.

A4 class No. 4468 Mallard, restored to her former glory and remaining in pristine condition at the National Railway Museum at York. *Don Hale*

Mallard hauls a railtour chartered train out of Scarborough station in 1986. *Milepost 92 ½*

The resting place of Sir Nigel Gresley. He was buried in April 1941 next to his wife's grave and within the family plot, beneath the Boscobel Oak at Netherseale in Derbyshire. *Don Hale*

bearings had been torn from the faces – sign of a serious problem. The white metal was designed to wear, but tearing suggested that the lubrication wasn't working, or that part of the axle was about to suffer a critical failure. Following discussions with Gresley, however, Bulleid issued instructions for the support team to return home, since the agreed testing period of three weeks had already been extended to ten.

Bulleid believed that the different examination techniques, combined with the hard French test rollers, might have contributed to some of the locomotive's damage and unreliability. Before returning to Doncaster, however, the LNER accepted Chapelon's invitation to show *Cock o' the North* at a prestigious railway exhibition in the centre of Paris. It was a major publicity coup for the French CME and a welcome boost for Gresley after the series of disappointments during the tests. On 17 February 1935, the stylish British engine was admired by hundreds of thousands of visitors at Gare du Nord, together with the latest Nord Pacific locomotives. Two years later, in 1937, both *Cock o' the North* and other P2s were rebuilt.

Gresley's chief draughtsman, Barney Symes, remembered his own excitement and interest whilst working on test with this particular locomotive. He later recalled in the *Gresley Observer*, the magazine of the Gresley Society:

> When *Cock o' the North* was on the boards, Gresley was a frequent visitor to the office, often accompanied by Oliver Bulleid, then his personal assistant. I was too junior to be in at any time on the discussions except when it really concerned my job. There was an occasion of this sort when I proposed a larger piston crosshead and gudgeon pin as I found the bearing pressure due to larger cylinders and shorter connecting rods rendered the standard crosshead inadequate.
>
> Gresley said to me: 'Why have you done this?' but after studying the figures gave his approval. When we were testing the engine, it was a gudgeon pin that ran hot. This, however, was due

to the hit and miss lubrication on a fault that was corrected in later years. I rode on the front of the engine with a senior draughtsman to take the indicator diagrams showing the steam action in the cylinders.

There was a wooden shelter to prevent us from falling off but it was very hot beside the smoke box and on the cylinders. When not indicating we stood up with our backs to the smoke box door and it was quite a pleasant ride – in fact much better than in the cab.

Gresley met us at King's Cross on each trip and examined our diagrams – which were rather dirty – and also the dynamometer car records. I remember him telling the driver: 'Don't go faster down the banks – run faster up them.' We had been touching 80mph on the Essendine bank between Stoke Summit and Peterborough.

At much the same time that Gresley's LNER team were conducting new brake trials with *Cock o' the North*, mayhem was breaking out once more on the streets of Nazi Germany. By the Night of the Long Knives in June 1934, when he purged the Nazi Party of those he considered a threat to his authority, Hitler had cemented his iron grip on every aspect of German life. There was increasing trouble at home in Britain, too. By March 1935, the government was concerned about the health of the nation, with hunger seriously affecting workers, and soup kitchens a common sight on major city streets. Oswald Mosley's Blackshirts were rampant in several hard-hit areas, frequently clashing with rival political and ethnic groups. The north of England had been particularly hard hit but marches and protests were common everywhere. In south Wales, a communist-led Workers' Movement march mobilised some 300,000 protestors at a single demonstration.

In the midst of all these problems, a new set of high-speed brake tests for LNER were scheduled. It was agreed that 5 March would be the date to compete and make comparisons with the German diesel railcar proposal. The locomotive, A3 class No. 2750, *Papyrus*, would operate between London and Newcastle, hauling seven coaches including the dynamometer car. Like many other LNER locomotives, the engine was named after a racehorse.

King's Cross driver Gutteridge drove the engine on the 'down' leg. He ran well at first with the seven coaches on a four-hour schedule and at times exceeded 88.5mph, covering the 268.3 miles journey in 237 minutes. On the return 'up' leg, the experienced Bill Sparshatt was again invited to 'run hard' past Grantham, where he set a fantastic new world record speed of 108mph coming down Stoke Bank. In total, operators claimed the locomotive had travelled over 300 miles that day at 80mph or more. The overall timings were 38 minutes faster than the German proposal and heralded a major victory for steam – defeating the German railcar proposal in terms of speed, weight, and potentially the increased number of passengers carried. The successful results of the LNER trials throughout 1934 and 1935 revived national interest and pride and advanced the belief that Gresley could and would do even better.

However, Gresley's joy at winning another world record was slightly subdued and it soon became clear that his mind was already on other matters: he had prepared the blueprint for his proposed streamlined A4 class and was determined to persuade the board to endorse the development of this unorthodox and streamlined Pacific. Once again, Gresley and LNER faced a make or break situation. Reputation and funding were on the line. All the euphoria of the past few years would count for nothing if either the LMS or the Reichsbahn made a successful speed challenge and Gresley's A4s failed to live up to expectations. The success of *Papyrus* on 5 March gave Gresley a few more days to present his final argument to the board. He knew he would need all the support he could muster and, despite his typical optimism and confidence, must still have had all his fingers crossed when he attended the meeting.

Given that Europe was in turbulence, and Britain itself was facing so many problems, it seems odd that consideration was given to the production of a new luxury engine. Yet the moment seemed ripe for Gresley to do something special, and his grapevine must have been buzzing from the spring of 1935 onwards. His informants in France – including André Chapelon and Ettore Bugatti – all reported much activity on the German steam front. He was also aware of competition from Stanier, plus the other potential threat from lightweight diesel sets.

Gresley must have known that one day he must face the inevitable and bow to more modern technology. For the moment, however, he was still determined to prove his steam theory. He knew the board had to be convinced that his new Pacifics were capable of working a demanding four-hour schedule between London and Newcastle for a new and prestigious service. This proposed link had been identified by the LNER marketing team for promotion of an elite business section and was intended as a fast, luxurious service to complement its established 'Flying Scotsman' service.

Sometime during Gresley's initial design considerations, he had a sudden brainwave: he could capitalise on the forthcoming national celebrations for the twenty-fifth anniversary of King George V's ascending the throne. Just three days after the *Papyrus* success, William Whitelaw publicly promised Gresley a new streamlined service to run between London and Newcastle, and confirmed it would be called the 'Silver Jubilee'.

Gresley must have had a grin as wide as the Tyne when he heard the news, and again a week or so later, when he visited Doncaster works to talk with his colleagues to make urgent plans to introduce this new service using his long-awaited A4 designs. But perhaps his smile had worn a little thin by the end of the month; with final approval coming so late, he had only a limited amount of time to add the final touches to his design drawings. The 'Silver Jubilee' service was scheduled to start on 30 September 1935, and officials were left with just five months to complete the designs and build both the locomotives and new luxury coaches – a remarkably short time even then, and unimaginably so now.

It was standard company policy, dating back to GNR days, to order locomotives in batches of ten, but Gresley proposed building a mere four new locomotives, each capable of hauling a 220-ton load, and also suggested introducing a complete new set of seven luxury coaches. They would seat seventy-eight first class passengers and 120 third class passengers, and include the latest hi-tech equipment and facilities, air conditioning, an electric kitchen and separate restaurant cars for each class. With such a train, the LNER would gain an edge over its rivals, offering passengers the latest in design and comfort whilst claiming glory for the company with a unique tribute to the royal family. The icing on the cake would be the painting of both the engines and their carriages in an eye-catching silver livery. This had seldom been tried on the railway – not surprising given the dirt and grime steam locomotives produced. But if the cleaners could stay on top of their task, the result would look spectacular.

Gresley and his assistants had to use their many years of experience to ensure the new class contained all the latest modifications and improvements to get the very most out of its potential. The drawing office prepared the plans during the latter days of March and April, before Gresley visited Doncaster works again, this time with most of his King's Cross team, to outline the final requirements to senior staff and reiterate the importance of meeting the deadline.

Gresley pledged to make this most special passenger express train one of his most exciting ever, with revolutionary shapes and striking hues. It wasn't a case of simply picking colours from some chart, however. Ever the experimenter, Gresley tried several shades of grey and silver in a variety of paintwork on a small works shunting engine until inspiration finally arrived. The raw paperwork barely hints at Gresley's superb new design. The first production contract for the new A4 class was issued by LNER on order No. 338 for just four engines, all named for the royal anniversary. They were works number 1818 (running no. 2509) *Silver Link*; works number 1819 (running no. 2510) *Quicksilver*; works no. 1821 (running no. 2511) *Silver King*; and finally works no. 1823 (running no. 2512) *Silver Fox*.

Silver Link was to be the first trial engine and would be painted in an unusual and unorthodox livery, with its smokebox casing in dark charcoal grey, and the side, skirting and frames in battleship grey. The remainder would be silver grey without any linings. The exterior livery of the coaches would be silver grey, with a chromium trim, and incorporated rubber sheeting between the carriages to maintain the streamlining effect and to help reduce wind resistance.

When the new A4s were first proposed, the financial situation was vastly different from the old days. The whole country was in recession and funds were extremely tight. The CME wanted only a limited number of prototype engines to work the 'Silver Jubilee' service. He knew they would face a very stern examination and did not want to commit further company funds to the scheme in case it failed. The workshop deadline, too, was very tight. By the time all the paperwork had been completed, the Doncaster engineers had only eleven weeks to construct the first locomotive and all the carriages. This batch of four A4s was ordered very late in LNER's financial year and only just made the budget programme.

In June, however, despite the rush and urgency of the project, Gresley took time out from all this chaos to visit his friend Bugatti in Paris and compare notes. For his new Pacifics, Gresley had in mind something very different in appearance from conventional steam locomotives. He must have been thinking of a radical new shape many months before the unprecedented success of both *Flying Scotsman* and *Papyrus*. He had already discussed and modified his preliminary drawings with engineering colleagues, and in principle had gained the approval of Wedgwood – but everyone involved realised the importance of the board's next decision.

Between 1928 and 1935, Gresley had produced some of the finest British locomotives in history. They were sleek, attractive, versatile, powerful and, above all, fast. Their performances had constantly taken on and beaten all comers out of sight. But Gresley had no desire to rest on his laurels. His association with Bugatti and his use of unusual horizontal wedge-shaped front ends had attracted criticism from a number of German and United States railway experts. Although LNER executives put much of this down to sheer jealousy, Gresley was aware of the controversy. He knew his main critics were strong advocates of the rival vertical wedge design which pushed air along the sides of trains rather than over the top – which we now know is flawed because the side of a train is the biggest generator of aerodynamic drag.

Well-known American industrial designers Raymond Loewy and Henry Dreyfuss fuelled the overseas criticism, preferring their own streamlined designs for cars, trains and ocean liners. A few years before, Loewy had said Bugatti's French railcars displayed 'unsophisticated streamlining' (whatever that means), adding that they had 'poor aerofoil' and were 'lacking in grace'. Surely this was sour grapes from a man whose designs, whilst elegant, never achieved the heights that Gresley's streamliners were to do.

Other critics blamed Chapelon and Gresley for sharing ideas and believed both had used techniques first developed on their own US engines. Despite this hullabaloo, however, Gresley finally won the day again at King's Cross: the board supported his ambitious proposals and agreed to invest in this radical new rolling stock. The ball was now rolling.

For the men and women in the Doncaster works, the next few months would prove to be an exhilarating time. Many former staff recalled that their happiest time in the works and drawing office was during that hectic, exciting period when the A4s were first being produced.

Not everything went to plan, however. There was a three-quarter-scale wooden mock-up of the shape for use in the wind tunnel. When Gresley came into the office, he picked up a draughtsman's pencil and drew the line of the footplate on the side of it, curving down to the front alongside the smokebox and down to the cab.

For once, Gresley's penchant for impromptu design didn't quite work – the rear portion was not very clear and the chief draughtsman at the time thought he had requested a straight slope. Drawings were made accordingly and the blacksmiths had the angle irons on the frame the following week.

Then, Barney Symes later recalled, suddenly there was a crisis: Gresley wanted the chief draughtsman in the erecting shop at once.

> He was told: 'I don't want this, Broughton! I want a curve like an aeroplane wing.' The chief draughtsman returned with a long face, and the team started the curve of the valance with the help of a curve from an airship copied from an engineering magazine.
>
> It was drawn up by two of us on wooden planks clipped to the offending angle irons. The smiths took it from there for the first engine while a new drawing was made, agreeing as far as possible with this curve for the next engines. The shape of the smoke box was drawn many times before Gresley was finally satisfied.

The frame was laid for No. 2509, *Silver Link*, at Doncaster on 26 June 1935, and just seventy-six days later the engine left the Doncaster works for trials. Gresley's Pacifics always created a sensation when first introduced, and *Silver Link*, with her dazzling livery and extraordinary shape, more dart than tube, proved no exception.

Pressure to produce the remaining engines was now intense. *Quicksilver* had her frame laid on 15 July, some nineteen days after

Silver Link — and left the works on 21 September, just two weeks after her sister engine. *Silver King* left Doncaster works on 5 November, and *Silver Fox* on 18 December.

Silver Link had two weeks of trials, including speed and brake tests, and attracted generous publicity from the LNER PR department for about ten days before Gresley arranged a very unusual public press run, just days before the start of the new service. The press releases confirmed production details of *Silver Link* and her sister engines and highlighted the many benefits of the luxury coaches and high-speed service. They said the locomotive had already achieved speeds of 100mph on test and suggested tremendous potential.

The VIP acceptance tickets were soon snapped up and the guest list included Bulleid, Gresley himself, Cecil J. Allen, and Randolph Churchill, son of Winston, who was covering the event for the *Daily Mail*. The chief general manager, Sir Ralph Wedgwood, also agreed to host a special luncheon, and the whole of Fleet Street, together with the wider public, watched and waited in anticipation.

On 27 September 1935, A4 Pacific No. 2509, *Silver Link*, left Platform 6 at King's Cross with a spectacular haul of seven brand-new, super-luxury 'Silver Jubilee' coaches bound for a special round trip to Grantham. For the benefit of the press it was officially called a 'demonstration' run. At the regulator was A. Taylor, a top shed driver from King's Cross. He had ably followed the example of his predecessors, Tommy Toplis, Ben Glasgow and Bill Sparshatt, and on this occasion was assisted by his fireman J. Luty. The VIP passengers were treated to a grand lunch with wine and full trimmings by Sir Ralph Wedgwood. Surprisingly, and despite all the pre-publicity, Wedgwood unexpectedly put a slight dampener on the event, playing down the role of *Silver Link* during an after-lunch speech and claiming that no particular record attempt was planned.

His speech echoed some of the similar puzzling comments made a few months earlier by his boss, company chairman William Whitelaw, about the unsuitability of the East Coast line for speed trials. It all added to the confusion, but possibly Gresley had a hand in the speech, as he had seemed a little annoyed by the continual boasting from the LNER press office. While he obviously shared everyone's hopes of further speed success, these press claims only added more pressure and he was certainly never one to shout about his own ambitions from the rooftops. Perhaps, though, the train crew was better aware of the real plan. Just before *Silver Link* left King's Cross, the stewards diligently removed the vases of cut flowers from the tables in anticipation of an interesting journey.

The demonstration journey was recorded by Cecil J. Allen, the LNER official and railway journalist. He occupied a window seat in the leading brake third compartment where he intended to record the performance undisturbed. However, his best-laid plans soon fell apart when he was quickly joined by Randolph Churchill and then by Gresley, who took his seat along with Charles Brown, the line's civil engineer. Mr Brown became slightly alarmed as the journey progressed, especially when they hurtled through Hitchin in Hertfordshire at 107mph, and rattled through the next twenty-seven miles in just fifteen minutes – a speed of 108mph. It seemed that VIP passengers were having their bubbly shaken rather than stirred and, according to ex-shed master and former LNER official P.N. Townend, a sharp exchange of words took place between Gresley and the driver on the footplate. Apparently Gresley travelled via the corridor tender to tell Taylor he was going too fast, saying: 'Ease your arm young man, we have twice touched 112mph.' This apparently astonished the driver, who said the speed recorder was not operating properly and only indicated a speed of 90mph. Gresley responded: 'Go a bit easier, we have an old director in the back and he is getting a bit touchy.'

Taylor fortunately slowed for the notorious Offord curves (probably still believing he was only doing about 70mph). On falling gradients from Stevenage, the engine maintained high speeds of more than 100mph for over 25 miles and achieved a new British record speed of 112.5mph on two separate occasions, at Ardsley and Sandy, both on level tracks.

It was later found that the driver had been right: the cab indicator was indeed broken and only went up to 90mph. Taylor also admitted that one of the inspectors had told him the boiler pressure was too low in the climb from King's Cross and ordered the fireman to redouble his efforts. He added: 'I didn't think we'd been going much above 90mph and apparently it was smoother on the engine than the train.'

Apart from a bit of turbulence, the trial was a huge success, exceeding all the company's expectations. It was the highest ever speed achieved on a former Great Northern line. It all seemed very promising for the mainline service which was due to commence a couple of days later. Gresley must have been delighted; on the locomotive's return to King's Cross he was photographed excitedly talking and congratulating the driver, proudly waving his large stopwatch at colleagues to declare 112mph.

To say the run caused a sensation is an understatement: this was the fastest anyone had travelled by rail in Britain. One reporter described his trip in vivid terms: 'Shooting and winding through the countryside like a silver snake and charging with its head down.' Another paper claimed that driver Taylor was 'not particularly sooty after the double journey'. What it said about the fireman is, sadly, unrecorded.

But if the acid test of a steam locomotive was what the crews think of it, Gresley had little to worry about. Taylor, who was later awarded the OBE for his achievement, was euphoric: '*Silver Link* is the finest engine we have ever had. There is no vibration whatsoever. We could easily have gone faster if we had wanted to – and we were not all-out by any means.' LNER drivers were never normally encouraged to travel at speeds this high, and Taylor must have loved the opportunity to see just how fast this new locomotive could go. The results of the trial proved a much-needed boost to morale, both within the LNER and across the country at large. With the German presence looming menacingly over Europe, it suddenly seemed possible that a blow could be dealt to its growing supremacy.

Chapter Eight
The Germans Increase the Pressure

n 10 October 1935, German Railways announced details of successful tests of their new steam locomotive, 05.002. The immediate results proved only speculative, but Gresley was determined to find out the true details. According to his informants, the trials had actually started months before and the Reichsbahn only went public when they had an authenticated speed record to boast about.

The latter part of the 1930s became a time of major change for most European railway networks. In Germany, the new lightweight diesel sets regularly hogged the headlines, often to the detriment of steam, and observers predicted that the latter faced a battle to survive and a limited future. As in Britain, steam trains still had a reputation for being dirty, noisy and smelly, and engineers faced an uphill battle to convince management of the need to invest in new steam development. What pushed the balance in steam's favour was a presumption that steam locomotives might soon be needed for other duties and that their engines would need to be more powerful.

Fortunately, enough significant people remained convinced of their potential, including Dr Wagner, the head of traction for the Reichsbahn, his chief designer Adolf Wolff, and Friedrich Witte, a promising young mechanical engineer who had recently returned from studying steam locomotive production and testing in America. Like André Chapelon and Gresley, Witte shared an interest in the massive Mikados operating on the New York Central line and enthused about a new system to create additional power with efficiently stored superheat (later introduced on the new German 05 class under test).

Among the key officials who endorsed the need for a new breed of engine that was both powerful and fast, the most notable was Dr Richard Wagner. Born in Berlin on 25 August 1882, Wagner had been a student of Robert Garbe, Prussian Railways' chief mechanical engineer, and later became chief engineer for Einheit's steam locomotives. He worked on the study of steam engineering at the Technical College in Berlin-Charlottenberg. In 1906, shortly after joining the Prussian Railways, he undertook study trips to both England and America. He later worked at the engine inspectorate in Wittenberg and then at the engine office No. 2, in Dortmund. Wagner became 'locomotive inspector' at the start of the war in 1914, based at the central railway office, Eisenbahn-Zentralamt in Berlin, and later served with the German military railway service.

Following the end of hostilities, he supervised the abolition of the military railway service and in 1920 was responsible for the Berlin-Grunewald locomotive test centre. Just two years later, he became head of the locomotive department at the central office in Berlin. Wagner was also a member of the locomotive standardisation committee and, in 1928, he was made chairman and later received an honorary degree from the Technical College at Aachen.

Much to the disapproval of Nazi officials, many of the German engineers and designers continued their friendships with British railway officials, and, unlike some of their political counterparts, willingly shared and discussed details of developments and speed tests. There was obvious rivalry, but they had mutual respect for each other. A fluent English speaker, Wagner was a friend of both Gresley and Bulleid and an old acquaintance of Harold Holcroft and William Stanier. He was even a member of the British Royal Society, and an honorary member of the Association of British Locomotive Engineers and Institution of Locomotive Engineers.

Wagner, too, wanted to exploit his own streamlining theories, promoting a series of trials on coal-fired, three-cylinder 4-6-4 designs. They ran well but, like Gresley, Wagner was a stubborn man and convinced they could do even better. He believed his designs would eventually solve the problem of hauling heavy-duty trains on the Berlin to Hamburg line – the same route as the Maybach-powered *Flying Hamburger* units.

The Germans built several steam prototypes between 1931 and 1935, with officials claiming that competition between the very different steam and electric trains would stimulate further interest and generate fierce competition. They also wanted to throw down a specific challenge to other European designers and, to a certain extent, wished to toe the party line by proving that German engineering was still the best. The Third Reich, ever keen to promote new propaganda and new technological achievements, readily supported the programme.

In February 1935, Dr Wagner visited London to present a paper to the Institution of Locomotive Engineers, with Gresley in the chair. Entitled 'High Speed and the Steam Locomotive', Wagner's report was mainly concerned with his theories on the benefits of streamlining. It generated considerable interest, and Wagner then invited a British delegation to visit Berlin the following year to sample life on a 'demonstration' high-speed steam run with his latest test engine.

The Germans wanted to dominate the European travel market and worked solidly on improving both locomotives and quality of rolling stock. Initial tests with a type 03 proved invaluable and in May 1935 Wagner introduced two new locomotives especially designed for high-speed working. They were the 4-6-4-type 05 class, No. 001 and No. 002, designed by Wolff at the Borsig factory in Berlin.

The first two members of the locomotive class were near identical. According to the records, locomotive 05 class No. 002 first appeared in a maroon livery and bore some resemblance to a large rhinoceros in shape, with a streamlined body and boiler and skirting above the wheels. No. 001 and No. 002 were coal-fired and the reports claim the fireman had to shovel coal at the rate of three tonnes per hour. There was also a No. 003, a completely different type of engine, which mainly used coal dust as fuel.

The sources (enthusiasts' memories as well as official records) differ slightly in their account of the precise details but indicate that this class of engine generated extraordinary power using a secret and experimental 'Kesselsieve' system of stored superheat within the boiler. This apparently boosted normal power significantly when required and enhanced high-speed running. Some engineers claimed the boiler was liable to suffer from occasional leaking tubes and firebox, and during the record run the following year some passengers apparently said the train vibrated and the locomotive 'shook like a wild horse'.

The first preliminary trials started in June 1935 and attracted as guest passengers many high-profile people from the armed forces and Third Reich. Speed trials from October onwards produced some incredible results and the engines were exhibited at various celebrations marking the centenary of the coming of the railway to Germany with Stephenson's locomotive.

According to records of German high-speed running, both No. 001 and No. 002 achieved consistently impressive timings on the Berlin to Hamburg route. Over the next year, many so-called propaganda runs took place. The first listing appears on 7 June 1935 and shows that 05 class No. 002's debut high-speed run achieved 191.7kmph/119.1mph with a 196-ton load between Paulinenaue and Nauen. A second run on 26 July, with 205 tons, achieved a new record of 195.7kmph/121.6mph, though many of these timings were not authenticated. Other officially published records showed 177.3kmph with 254 tons on 18 October 1935 and, on 5 February 1936, the locomotive registered 180.0kmph with 242 tons.

On 9 May 1936, the engine hauled another special train of VIP passengers, including many from the armed forces, among them several generals and four admirals. One particular name stood out, that of Admiral Heusinger-Waldegg, whose family had historic connections with the German railways. The actual speed achieved that day is uncertain as the run was not officially designed as a time trial or brake test, but simply staged to impress its passengers. Some anti-Nazi critics suggested, in underground newspapers now preserved in the German press archive, that these performances were designed to 'increase the glory of an obscure political system by displaying achievements pretended to be their own'. On the same day, Hitler celebrated with his fellow Fascist dictator Mussolini the successful invasion of Ethiopia.

On 11 May another propaganda run was arranged for top Nazi officials and Reichsbahn senior management, from Hamburg to a stop at Wittenberg, presumably for water, and then back to Berlin. Other test or propaganda trains ran about the same time and possibly even on the same days, highlighting a Doble steamcar, a Henschel-Wegman-Zug, and a high-speed diesel set. But this run was not just for display purposes; with drivers Langhams and Hoene on the footplate and railway engineers Roth and von Jagow in front, it culminated in a world record speed of 200.4kmph/124.5mph for a 197-ton train – 12mph faster than Gresley's then record.

Documents show the train actually set two records that day during the same journey. The locomotive achieved 178.2kmph just before the stop at Wittenberg, and then 200.4kmph near Paulinenaue. The Germans later admitted that it was their intention to achieve 200kmph at some point during that period. The dynamometer car tracing shows an outline gradient profile. It does not show the actual grades but indicates the rises and falls next to km distances. The record suggests that 05 class No. 002 had not reached its absolute limit and that most of the acceleration was carried out on level tracks with a small amount of downhill running. It also indicates the train reached or passed 110mph five times, beating 115mph four times and 120mph twice. Other records show the locomotive exceeded 110mph on eight occasions rather than five. The papers show the 200.4kmph maximum was achieved at km post 60, close to Friesack station on a level stretch of track, following acceleration after a climb from Neustadt Dosse and a long downhill stretch to around km post 63. The latter run must have been one of the fastest ever recorded in Europe behind steam. The return journey achieved an overall average speed of 81.15mph including a two-and-a-half-minute stop at Wittenberg.

As planned, a number of top Nazi Party and Reichsbahn officials witnessed the event. The official passenger list was approved and compiled by Joseph Goebbels and it was said that Herman Goering, then Minister of the Interior, wanted to travel but was unable to do so owing to a prior engagement with Hitler. Goering was a keen train enthusiast and kept a model railway with miniature rolling stock in his attic throughout the war years. In addition to the Reichsbahn engineers and officials, including Dr Wagner, Dr Nordmann and Dr Dorpmoller, the passenger list contained top Nazi officials Reinhard Heydrich and Heinrich Himmler. One wonders what they discussed during their long journey in the same compartment.

This steam record was acclaimed by Reich Propaganda Minister Goebbels as 'proof of German efficiency and good workmanship'. The achievement was the climax to more than a year of speed trials using the two super-powered locomotives and became an additional tool of a boastful Nazi publicity machine.

Following Dr Richard Wagner's invitation to British officials the year before, the British party finally accepted an invitation to travel on another special steam train, on 30 May 1936, less than three weeks after the German high-speed record was achieved. Cecil J. Allen attended along with Holcroft, Bulleid, Stanier and a host of other notable British guests, mainly railway officials, engineers and members of the Institution of Locomotive Engineers. Dr Wagner played host to his guests, accompanied by other

Reichsbahn officials, including Dr Dorpmoller. It is uncertain whether any Third Reich officials took part. They had endorsed the *Flying Hamburger* trip three years earlier, but attitudes had hardened since. Dr Wagner's friendship with the British engineers was now viewed with suspicion, and many in the higher reaches of the German government disapproved of the British visit.

Records show that on that day the train covered 250 miles at over 90mph, with William Stanier enjoying a spell on the footplate. Once again the locomotive produced another magnificent performance, achieving 118mph/190kmph – apparently without much effort. This was a relatively lightweight train of 145 tons but it may have incurred some problems on the return journey from Hamburg to Berlin. The notes show it took 130 minutes for the outward leg and more than three hours back with a stop at Wittenberg, where Cecil J. Allen took some photographs for his report.

Although the 05 class No. 002 received plaudits from foreign engineers, it did incur several maintenance faults and designers began to experiment with other varied prototypes. They studied Chapelon's refinement of steam passages, and adaptations to the water feed, and incorporated several other modifications with the aim of creating an even bigger and better locomotive, able to run harder and faster, and establish an unbeatable steam record.

Back in England, the new 'Silver Jubilee' service was proving popular and again achieved notable results, though the A4 locomotives were not required to travel at their fastest pace on the regular journey to and from Newcastle, registering an average speed of 67mph. *Silver Link* had had to work the service on her own for two weeks before the other locomotives in the same class became available. She completed thirteen successive round trips before she was finally relieved, covering an impressive 8000 miles without failure.

Silver Link did experience some running problems during her early days of service with the brick arch in her firebox collapsing. This was soon rectified but it meant urgent attention was required during the weekend after its first week of operation. The problem happened again on at least one other occasion and, during an overnight stop at Gateshead shed, the brick arch was partially repaired. However, there was not enough time to allow it to cool, and the repairs were carried out in dangerous conditions with unacceptably high temperatures, a practice allowed in America but banned in Britain – and for good reason. The brick arch is like a giant storage heater, easily capable of burning anyone near it. Fortunately, in this instance no one was injured, and the work was satisfactorily completed.

The A4 class No. 2510, *Quicksilver*, began high-speed running tests in early October 1935, and started work on the Newcastle run two weeks after *Silver Link*. No. 2511, *Silver King*, left Doncaster works on 5 November, and No. 2512, *Silver Fox*, departed on 18 December. All four engines performed well on tests and in service with the 'Silver Jubilee' train. However, *Silver Link* gained the most plaudits for her incredible debut run and for maintaining the service until the other engines were ready. On 20 January 1936, the first four A4s responsible for hauling the 'Silver Jubilee' were called together at King's Cross for a unique commemorative photograph. On that same evening, King George V, whose jubilee had been the spur for their creation, died at Sandringham.

Each weekday, the train left Newcastle at 10 a.m. and King's Cross at 5.30 p.m. with one stop at Darlington. Despite the fact that passengers had to pay a supplementary fare to travel on this high-speed service, the train always proved extremely popular, especially with businessmen, and nearly every seat was taken; advance bookings were usually essential. The average speed for the service was some 70.4mph and the train daily achieved running speeds of 90mph. Statistics showed the average number of passengers totalled 145 northbound, and 131 southbound.

Punctuality was always considered vital by the LNER management and the 'Silver Jubilee' always arrived at King's Cross between one and five minutes early. During the first two years of service the train was delayed on only two occasions, an extraordinary testimony to the professionalism of the LNER staff and the good workmanship of their locomotives. The first incident came on 4 September 1936, when an 'up' train with *Quicksilver* at the head overheated at York and an Atlantic had to be hastily mustered to draw the train, which reached King's Cross twenty-five minutes late. The second happened on 14 October, when *Quicksilver* failed again and driver Bill Sparshatt took over No. 4477 *Gay Crusader* in her place at Doncaster. Sparshatt, who had driven *Flying Scotsman* on her record-breaking run, was a regular top link driver, the highest rung of the professional ladder; this substitution came during his final week of service.

The outstanding success of the 'Silver Jubilee' service from September 1935 – and in particular *Silver Link*'s magnificent performance – put the country's railways back in the world spotlight again for all the right reasons, and impressed the British authorities. Its success finally persuaded the government to provide essential funding to LNER for future development of similar high-speed and upgraded rolling stock.

Satisfied with the performance of the service and its locomotives and with the welcome backing of a government loan, LNER directors soon approved another order for an additional ten similar locomotives. This was followed by a third order for another seven locomotives, and a further allowance was made for the production of a few other essential classes. The 1936 programme also permitted the replacement of some heavy-duty freight, shunting and express passenger engines, with most new locomotives produced in apple green or jet black.

Gresley's knowledge of his new class of A4s and the advancement of streamlining techniques persuaded him to make another attempt at the speed record on 27 August 1936, with the aim of improving on *Silver Link*'s record the previous September. This time, he used *Silver Link*'s sister engine *Silver Fox*, on an ordinary southbound express. The driver was told to 'open up' and achieved 113mph – another British record. However, the engine developed operational problems, with damage to the middle big end, which disintegrated. The cylinder end cover was also badly damaged but the run had set a second record, with the best speed ever recorded in the world for a revenue-earning train – and one that wouldn't be broken regularly in Britain until the 1970s. A week or so after this success, the LNER directors revised their programme for the construction of even more A4 Pacifics, bringing the total number to thirty-five.

The success of the 'Silver Jubilee' and the established 'Flying Scotsman' naturally encouraged LNER to consider additional high-speed options. A couple of years after the 'Silver Jubilee' service was launched, the company announced details of another similar high-speed train: 'Coronation', running between London and Edinburgh and designed to compete with rival services at William Stanier's LMS and to complement the LNER's own successful services. Following the example of the 'Silver Jubilee' locomotives, it again was named to mark a royal celebration: the coronation of King George VI, who had succeeded to the throne following the abdication of his elder brother Edward VIII. This time, the striking locomotives would appear in Bugatti's famous garter-blue racing livery with a wedge-shaped beaver-tail observation saloon at the rear, based on the design of his racing cars. The garter-blue colours were also applied to seven new Pacifics allocated to work on additional streamlined trains, which were introduced during 1937. *Silver Link* appeared in garter blue in December 1937 and this livery was later adopted as standard for the rest of the class. The new A4s also received a brass, chromium-plated nameplate. And once again, the royal link added prestige to the service, stimulating further public and press interest.

The board also discussed proposals to extend the 'Silver

Jubilee' service from London to Aberdeen, a distance of 524 miles. Provisional details had first been published in July 1936. The schedule saw the train depart King's Cross at 12.15 p.m., reach Newcastle in four hours, then stop for five minutes at Newcastle, and arrive two hours later in Edinburgh. There, the train would halt for fifteen minutes before continuing via Kirkcaldy, Arbroath and Montrose to Aberdeen, another two and three-quarter hours away. Even allowing for problems with gradients and a part single-track stretch, the journey from London to the Granite City would be accomplished well within nine hours. No scheduled train had run so fast north of Newcastle since the famous 'Races to the North' nearly forty years before.

A trial run for the 'Coronation' service was organised for 26 September 1936, using A4 'Silver Jubilee' stock. LNER operated a test run north from Newcastle to Edinburgh with the Gateshead reserve locomotive *Silver King* and the dynamometer car. The route to Edinburgh did not allow sustained high-speed working but the 255-ton train nevertheless enjoyed a run of 114 minutes out and 118 minutes back over the 124.4 mile journey to confirm a possible six-hour schedule from King's Cross to Edinburgh.

In the autumn of 1936, LNER confirmed plans to launch another high-speed service commencing in July 1937 to complement the 'Coronation', which by then had a revised schedule to include a new one-stop programme southbound from Edinburgh to London, and two halts northbound. The service, the 'West Riding Ltd', was planned as a luxury express to run between London and Leeds and Bradford. The two new A4 locomotives for this service were given names associated with the textile industry, *Golden Fleece* and *Golden Shuttle*. The press run took place on 23 September 1937, with A4 *Golden Fleece* running from Leeds to Barkston. The service on all of the high-speed trains was ultra-modern. Restaurant staff served meals at most seats and the coaches accommodated 168 third class passengers and forty-eight first class. From 1936 to the outbreak of war in 1939, *Silver Link* hauled 564 of the 1509 'Silver Jubilee' trains, thirty-two of the 'Coronation', and twelve of the 'West Riding Ltd'.

To meet demand on all of these new high-speed services, LNER authorised the construction of even more Pacific locomotives, all to be produced, as usual, at Doncaster works. The first six of these new locomotives appeared in apple-green livery, while the five new A4 locomotives selected to haul the 312-ton 'Coronation' servies were each painted to match the new coaches in a striking two-tone livery of garter blue and Marlborough blue. Some A4s were named after connections to the British Empire, including *Dominion of Canada* and *Union of South Africa*, and were used primarily on the 'Coronation' service for patriotic emphasis. Several other Pacifics had also appeared from Doncaster works from December 1936, together with two sets of 'Coronation' coaches that were available from the following May and June. They, too, initially had beaver-tail observation saloons (named for their shape, which was curved in a style reminiscent of a beaver's tail) at the rear of the train and consisted of nine special luxury coaches, articulated in four twin sets, with the observation saloon as the ninth.

LNER might be launching new luxury services to the north of Britain, but much of the country was still mired in poverty, with heavy unemployment and a succession of strikes that were devastating industry. Most of the population could not even contemplate riding on one of these trains and yet all seemed fully behind Gresley and his quest for the world speed record. The LNER management had a gift for understanding the mood of the moment. In October 1936 two hundred men from Jarrow, in the north of England, walked three hundred miles to London to bring public attention to the severe economic problems they faced. This crusade, which became known as the Jarrow Hunger

March, attracted substantial public sympathy, and LNER organised a special train to take the men back home. It was a perfectly judged gesture.

Chapter Nine
The LMS Draws Ahead

s the war drums were sounding in Europe, and Germany boasted about taking the steam record so easily, a chorus of shouts went up in Britain calling for an attempt to seize the record back. These came not only from the public, but also from the LMS offices at Euston station, just down the road from Gresley's office at King's Cross.

William Stanier believed Britain should fight back, and soon his senior staff were making loud noises that something might be imminent. In fact, Stanier was planning to issue a friendly challenge to Gresley and the LNER team: after his successes with his own powerful and impressive locomotives, he was determined to gain his own personal share of glory for high-speed running. He decided to throw a spanner in Gresley's plans by pushing his drivers and resources to the limit. Following on from the successful introduction of his first Pacific locomotive, *Princess Royal*, in 1936, Stanier decided to launch a new high-speed service of his own between London and Glasgow. Not only that, but it would be called the 'Coronation Scot', in direct competition with Gresley and his royal tributes.

LMS had always intended to develop a new locomotive that would modify and improve upon Stanier's earlier Princess designs. Taking a leaf out of Gresley's book, Stanier ensured that the nation was briefed about the launch of his new train and locomotive well in advance. Reporters and photographers were invited along to view the new engine and rolling stock under construction in Crewe works and drawings were released to newspapers and railway magazines. During June 1937, the new train was exhibited for public display for two days at Euston station. Using film coverage and rare appearances by veteran steam locomotives, LMS secured the use of the four-track section between Llandudno Junction and Colwyn Bay in north Wales to parade three historic trains in perfect parallel for the cameras. The camera and film unit were mounted on Stanier's new locomotive, No. 6220, *Coronation*.

Next, LMS organised a special press run on 29 June to promote their new 'Coronation Scot' train service with No. 6220. Some speculated that LMS would use this test to challenge the British steam record held by Gresley's LNER – and they were not wrong. With experienced driver Tom Clarke on the regulator, ably assisted by his fireman, John Lewis, the journey began well, with *Coronation* hauling eight new coaches for a 263-ton load on a round trip from London Euston to Crewe.

The team decided to try to attack the LNER record down Whitmore Bank. This was an eight-mile stretch of mixed gradients but had the disadvantage of approaching Crewe station from a reverse bend. The train worked well past Stafford and over Whitmore it touched 85mph. Gradually the speed rose to equal Gresley's before surpassing it, reaching 114mph before the brakes had to be slammed on hard. The train was approaching Crewe at more than 60mph and directed (for some unknown reason) towards Platform 3 by a reverse bend. Flames came shooting from the brake blocks and spectators gasped in horror as the express rattled over three crossover points on the station approaches.

Even the startled passengers, including seasoned recorders O.S. Nock and Cecil J. Allen, must have been alarmed as plates and bowls flew about the dining car, and passengers, observers and gentlemen of the press were hurled around the luxury carriages. Stanier's assistant, R.A. Riddles (later first chief mechanical engineer of British Railways), reported afterwards: 'The crockery in the dining car crashed. Down we came to 52mph through the curve with the engine riding like the great lady she is. There was not a thing we could do but hold on and let her take it. And take it she did.'

Despite the slight air of panic, everyone shared in the excitement and the great achievement of the day. The driver and fireman were congratulated on their efforts by the Crewe stationmaster, who was probably relieved he still had a station to master. The return journey was scheduled for 135 minutes for the 158 miles but 'Coronation Scot' arrived well within the two-hour schedule, to record an average speed of 79.7mph, including more than 72 miles at near 89mph, and another 100mph plus on the 'up' run.

Stanier had not only achieved his aim, of matching Gresley's success, but beat the latter's best time by just 1mph. He had finally secured a new high-speed British record for the LMS – but was still well short of the German steam world record of 124.5mph.

The press reaction was ecstatic. Much to Gresley's annoyance, journalists exaggerated the facts in their headlines the following day, some claiming that No. 6220 *Coronation* was 'the fastest in the world'. One report in the *Daily Express* ran with the heading 'British record 114mph' and claimed: 'On her record breaking run between Euston and Crewe, the new LMS *Coronation Scot* thundered past Watford at 70mph. Driver Tom Clarke estimated his speed at one point on the trip at 113mph. On the return journey from Crewe, she averaged 80mph and arrived 11 minutes ahead of schedule.'

William Stanier wasted no time in capitalising on his success: he soon announced that the 'Coronation Scot' service would operate in both directions from London to Glasgow, with a service leaving each station at 1.30 p.m. and reaching its destination at 8 p.m., with a two-minute stop for crew changes at Carlisle.

The success of his LMS rival must have acted like a red rag to a bull with Gresley. Apparently he began fidgeting nervously with his pipe when he heard the news, then immediately ordered his team to try and re-take the record the next day. He clearly knew in advance about Stanier's plans and had his own train crew waiting on standby. On 30 June he organised a demonstration press run, using his own 'Coronation' set, bedecked in Ettore Bugatti's beautiful garter-blue livery. The train, hauled by A4 class No. 4489, *Dominion of Canada*, had Gresley on board, with Cecil J. Allen, and Oliver Bulleid on the footplate.

The run journeyed from King's Cross to Barkston South Junction and back, turning on the triangle. On the outward leg of the journey, the train reached speeds in the 90s but on its return the King's Cross driver, Burfoot, pushed the locomotive to 109.5mph down Stoke summit. It was a valiant attempt, but still 4.5mph below the new LMS record. Gresley must have thought the attempt something of an anti-climax and it was a major disappointment, particularly after the furore of the previous day and Gresley's own earlier successes. A loss of boiler pressure at the crucial moment was blamed for the engine not being able to go that little bit extra. However, Gresley reacted only with a wry smile: he obviously had something else up his sleeve, and his supporters were convinced that he was keeping his powder dry until the time was right.

On 5 November 1937, the new LNER 'Coronation' luxury train finally came into service between London and Edinburgh. The 'Coronation' left King's Cross every weekday at 4 p.m. with a stop at York, arriving at Waverley station at 10 p.m. The overall average speed was 65.5mph for the 392.7 miles journey and the average speed between London and York was slightly higher at 71.9mph. The Edinburgh 'up' train left at 4.30pm with a scheduled stop at Newcastle. From there, it was just under four hours to King's Cross.

The 'Coronation' had a much tougher task than the 'Silver Jubilee' service, with an additional 124.4 miles leg each way from Newcastle to Edinburgh (in the summer a beaver-tailed observation saloon was added to the train to increase passenger enjoyment of the scenery). LNER's other new service, the 'West Riding' to Bradford and Leeds, began on 27 September 1937, using A4 Pacifics. The train left King's Cross at 7.10 p.m. and took just 2 hours and 40 minutes non-stop to Leeds, averaging 68.4 mph. This train was almost identical in service to the 'Coronation' but later travelled without the observation saloon, which proved too difficult to reverse out of Leeds station. The same livery was used, but because of heavy workings between the two Yorkshire towns running times suffered somewhat and the service was unreliable.

Meanwhile the Germans were suffering mixed fortunes in the transport field. Hitler's prestige building programme came to fruition in the late spring of 1936, just in time for the showpiece Olympic Games in Berlin. The new tunnel, built by the Reichsbahn to link the northern and southern electric suburban services, was officially opened a week before the start of the Games (another new north–south link-line ran from Stettiner Bahnhof to Unter den Linden). Nazi propaganda claimed the new network gave visitors to the Games a unique demonstration of German technology, with their S-Bahn services operating at intervals as short as ninety seconds and offering on average thirty-eight trains a day in each direction. The second part of the system took another three years to complete and finally came into service during the war.

A propaganda triumph to equal that of the world steam record had been their 1936 launch of the airship *Hindenburg*, which had shared secret testing facilities with several of Gresley's engineering associates in Germany. Weighing 236 tons, the *Hindenburg* could cruise at a speed of 80mph and travel unaided for up to six days, and it began a series of transatlantic flights, carrying passengers from Germany to America in luxurious conditions. Then, in May 1937, the *Hindenburg* crashed on landing at Lakehurst, New

Jersey, killing thirty-five of the ninety-seven people on board. It was a massive blow for the Nazi regime.

In October 1937 the trains reached the headlines again when Hitler greeted a special train to Berlin carrying the newly married Duke and Duchess of Windsor, formerly Edward VIII and Mrs Simpson. It was a tremendous political coup for Hitler, and Goebbels' publicity machine ensured maximum coverage. But on the technological front the news was less encouraging. The Germans' great hope was the Henschel V8, locomotive No. 19.001, the brainchild of Friedrich Witte, who was in charge of testing and development for the Deutsche Reichsbahn at Minden.

Witte had overseen the development of several American engines during a work-study period in the United States and shared the Nazi ideal of building an engine capable of winning and keeping the world steam record. The blueprint for his new engine, designed by Richard Roosen of Henschel & Sons, was first submitted in 1933, with a firm proposal agreed in 1935. Originally, it boasted a 4-6-2 Pacific wheel arrangement but this was later changed to a 2-8-2. Wagner made considerable input with his streamlining ideas and hoped that the overall efficiency of his engine would compensate for any increase in maintenance costs.

The locomotive contained an unusual and complicated V-shaped design mechanism using eight cylinders arranged in four pairs, and looked slightly similar in appearance to Gresley's A4 Pacifics. It took several years, however, to fully develop and modify and although Roosen claimed No. 19.001 eventually exceeded the 1936 German steam record of No. 05.002 on special test rollers – achieving a recorded 125mph – it failed to repeat the same performance on the track. Reports say the engine ran very well during brake tests and produced some superb displays, even recording 117mph on a test track with 'quiet running', but it later developed some technical problems. The engine also required far more maintenance than conventional steam engines and, owing to production difficulties and the volatile situation within Germany, it was not delivered to the Deutsche Reichsbahn until July 1941. By that time Witte had gone on to replace Dr Wagner, who had retired, to become head of the central railway office.

On 9 and 10 November, Berlin suffered another horrific day of violence and riots against ethnic minorities, resulting in the infamous Night of the Broken Glass. In March 1938, Adolf Hitler ordered the German army to occupy neighbouring Austria, where they proclaimed a union, something that had been explicitly forbidden by the Treaty of Versailles in 1919. Later that year, the Deutsche Reichsbahn took control of the rail networks of Austria, Sudetenland, Bohemia and Moravia.

Later in 1938, the 'Silver Jubilee' service again expanded, adding yet another coach to meet demand, but the train was still lighter than the 'Coronation' and 'West Riding'. 'Coronation''s new schedule now allowed for an additional stop at Newcastle. Despite increasing economic and political problems at home, the introduction and development of these luxury high-speed services created tremendous interest, providing much-needed employment for areas hard hit by the economic recession.

Gresley's former chief draughtsman, Barney Symes, later recalled some of the halcyon days at Doncaster, working on the 'Coronation' and 'West Riding' developments, when the world seemed to be constantly watching and waiting for news of events in Germany. But they also seemed to be waiting with almost equal anticipation for the latest masterpiece to emerge from the Doncaster sheds.

Symes later recalled:

Gresley took great interest in carriage design and décor, which is not surprising as he first came to the Great Northern to be carriage and wagon superintendent. When the *Coronation* train set came out for its trial run, we saw it go by from the office windows.

To our amazement, the end doors of each coach were emblazoned with lions 'or rampant' – as if this was a heraldic train. The office joker called out: 'Oh look, the circus is in town!' The chief draughtsman overheard this remark and immediately informed the mechanical engineer, who passed it on to Gresley. The lions never roared again!

By the late 1930s, the LNER's spectacular A4 locomotives were well known throughout the world as a symbol of luxury, speed and sheer power. For more than a decade the British public had held Nigel Gresley in awe, always waiting with anticipation to witness the launch of yet another of his new luxury train services, or to acknowledge the introduction of another colourful new locomotive. From the first, the A4s' distinctive sleek and streamlined appearance had proved an instant attraction with the public and crowds often waited three or four deep on mainline platforms when Gresley's engines first appeared, packing every possible vantage point to catch a glimpse of the new star attraction.

Gresley's success reflected the mood of the nation, and endorsed an overwhelming public desire to push high-speed travel to the limit. Everyone knew it was dangerous – but so were the times. It was as if the public recognised it was a case of now or never: war was looming. The public's response to the ongoing battle for speed certainly mirrored the attitude of the day, which could be summed up as 'give it our best shot', and was aimed at showing Germany who was boss.

Although Gresley had long dreamed of designing, developing and constructing a locomotive capable of both high speed and power, his focus had always been the requirements of the company – predominantly engines that could function as all-round workhorses to meet the demands of heavy express passenger and freight services; the records show that even up to 1937, LNER's main source of revenue was still as a carrier of freight rather than passengers. Constantly hampered by a limited budget and stern briefs from his board, Gresley's hands were tied. He could only build a minimal number of engines per year and his priority was always both low maintenance and low running costs. He had achieved astonishing things with his A4 class, but building a loco-motive that would beat not only the LMS but also the German speed record must have seemed like mission impossible.

The A4 class engine was, of course, the result of years of experimentation and research, and could not have happened without the experience of key staff members, including its star drivers. LNER enthusiasts Leslie Burley and Eric Neve both agree that driver Bill Sparshatt, in particular, contributed greatly to the success of the A4s, working hard during speed runs and generally helping the engine's advancement. Sparshatt finally retired in 1936 at the age of sixty-four, when his last run brought No. 4472 and the 8 a.m. 'up' train from Newcastle to London King's Cross. In the *Railway Magazine*, someone once wrote after seeing his portrait, 'the calmest face of William Sparshatt appeals as that of a man who has mastered the locomotive and has raised the footplate by walking worthily in the vocation to which he was called'.

Admirers of Gresley's A4 class also handed plaudits to Sir Ralph Wedgwood for his support, together with chairman William Whitelaw. They also praised the publicity efforts of Cecil J. Allen (and his informative reports), and of Teasdale and Dan-dridge in the PR department. Allen should not be forgotten; it was his job to make comparisons with other speed trials and he was a frequent traveller not only on the LNER runs but also on many rival ventures, and his actions kept LNER in the loop of vital information. As well as attending at least one of the German trials in May 1936, behind locomotive 05.002, he was invited by Gresley to accompany him on the trial run of 'Coronation', and was also a regular visitor to the LMS down the road at Euston, recording the drama at Crewe when LMS took the British title once more in the continuous cat and mouse chase for glory.

Gresley kept a close eye on all overseas developments, particularly in Germany, determined to look after the LNER's interests by keeping pace with his rivals. Another LNER enthusiast and Gresley Society supporter, Michael Joyce, believes that although Gresley had been impressed by high-speed trains in Germany and France, which were diesel-hauled and lightweight, he was still absolutely convinced that similar services could be introduced using steam engines.

The public remained fascinated by Nigel Gresley and his futuristic creations. He had already received many public honours, including an honorary degree of Doctor of Science from Manchester University, and had been elected president of the Institution of Locomotive Engineers. It was well known that he loved experimenting and that he always worked on the basis of trial and error. He possessed a naturally investigative mind and a highly competitive spirit but was a true professional who was always striving to improve. Gresley had built his engines and rolling stock on limited finances in order to meet his company's needs but at the same time had provided customers with exactly what they wanted: a fast and reliable service with first-class comfort and facilities.

Over the years Gresley had never disappointed his admirers, and his regular long-haul passenger expresses were often fully booked – in spite of LNER charging a premium rate. Gresley had become an icon of his era: it seemed the press and public loved him equally and hung on his every word. His public utterances, however, were limited, since he was a very private man and seemed to prefer the LNER publicity department and his own inventions to speak for him.

Gresley's standing in the engineering community was such that railways were not his sole concern. In 1935 he was asked to be chairman of a special committee set up by Sir Walter Runciman, President of the Board of Trade, in response to the recent sinking of two British steamships on the high seas: the *Usworth* and the

Blairgowrie, both of which foundered as a result of damaged steering gear. Gresley and his colleagues had the task of investigating the steering gear and making suggestions for improvements. As a result of this work, combined with all his other achievements in the field of British technology, Gresley received a knighthood in 1936.

On 26 November 1937, Gresley was awarded what to him may have been an even greater honour. Senior railway officials, together with past and present members of the LNER management team and notable engineers from across the nation, gathered at London's Marylebone Station. Those present included Francis Wintour, A.H. Peppercorn, Bert Spencer, Sir Ralph Wedgwood, Edward Thompson and Oliver Bulleid, all men steeped in railway tradition and history, and they had come to pay tribute to the work of the man they called the 'grand master'. There the hundredth A4 class Pacific, No. 4498, was officially named in his honour: *Sir Nigel Gresley*.

Chapter Ten
Mallard **Spreads Her Wings**

n 1937 Gresley's friend and assistant, Oliver Bulleid, left to become CME of the Southern Railway, leaving Gresley at the helm alone. For the LNER, it marked the end of a remarkable era. But it was not the end of the company's triumphs; in fact the greatest was about to come.

The next batch of A4 Pacifics, though ostensibly the same as the first batches, incorporated some important developments to make the most of the design's possibilities. They were each named after birds, a decision made by Gresley that no doubt revived happy memories from his time at Salisbury Hall, where he first developed his love of breeding wild birds. Eventually he built two small islands at the property, plus a shallow moat, designed to protect and develop his rare species. Gresley was so proud of his friendly wildfowl that he allowed his family to photograph him feeding them.

A.E. Beresford, a clerk at Gresley's King's Cross office, later reported that Gresley wrote down the name *Mallard* on the back of an envelope or on a sheet of paper, along with other suggestions such as *Guillemot*, *Herring Gull*, *Wild Swan*, *Gannet* and *Seagull*. Beresford said these were all British birds that were 'strong on the wing', to reflect the locomotives' speed and power. All of these names were given to new A4 Pacifics, but it was *Mallard* that proved to be Gresley's favourite and, according to reports, he either circled or underlined it at the top of the list.

Perhaps it was fondness for the species that caused him to place *Mallard* at the top of the list of the latest batch of locomotives under construction. Certainly from the first this particular engine seemed to receive preferential treatment and remained of special significance to him. It was rapidly upgraded with all the very latest modifications, including streamlined air passages and an increase in boiler and cylinder pressure, with the additional benefit of the new Westinghouse QSA brake valves and a Kylchap double chimney. This chimney had been specially tested in trials during 1937 by A3 No. 2751, *Humorist*, to ensure it was suitable for adaptation for the latest A4s. *Mallard* was completed in March 1938, exactly three years after the first order was endorsed by the LNER board for the first four Silver A4s. Much had been learnt during those years and all this information provided a tremendous opportunity for further improvements.

In view of recent near misses and other serious incidents, Gresley was concerned that the increasing speed of his locomotives meant that much longer braking distances were urgently required. He knew that his rivals at LMS, and elsewhere in the country, were busily designing or testing new prototypes. He was determined to critically examine the new Westinghouse vacuum brake system and was already examining a range of additional signalling systems. At the time, there was still no automatic signalling available throughout the East Coast workings. Gresley was a member of a government committee for automatic train control and railway electrification and therefore had a dual role, if not a vested interest, in safety matters.

Mallard first appeared on order No. EO342 in November 1936, receiving the works number 1870 and the LNER running number 4468, and costing a total of £8,500 to build. She became the first of four new locomotives to be fitted with the latest impressive state-of-the-art chimney and blastpipe, which allowed the exhaust smoke to be distributed more freely. These alterations to the blastpipe – the outlet for steam used in the cylinders – were critical. If the blastpipe is too small – imagine replacing a car's exhaust pipe with a pinhole-sized outlet – not enough gas can escape, which strangles the engine's power. But if it's too big, the gas leaves the engine while it still has energy that could be used to boost power. Getting it right is a fine balancing act and can only be achieved by lengthy experimentation – which is exactly what Gresley and his team had been doing for many years.

They also wanted to improve the streamlined shape still further. Although the A4s had all been thoroughly examined and improved, and now included Bugatti's wedge-shaped streamlining design, dispersing smoke from the chimney at the front of a locomotive remained a major problem, particularly on Pacifics, which had only a very small viewing window. For those on the footplate to have a good view of what they were doing was essential, especially at high speeds, and the issue worried Gresley intensely. The last thing he wanted was a major accident and loss of life.

Over the years Gresley and his team had visited the National Physical Laboratory at Teddington and other similar establishments in France run by André Chapelon in an attempt to find the perfect solution, but in vain. Solving this problem had frustrated not only Gresley but some of the best brains in the world, for decades. The issue had been a thorn in Gresley's side for years and success could just give him the edge over his rivals – and allow him to register a world-beating patent. The latest A4s now contained all the best of his previous experiments and modifications, and the smoke issue now seemed the last stubborn obstacle. The first wind-tunnel experiments dated back to the Wright Brothers in their aviation quest of 1903, and further extensive tests had been completed at the Zeppelin works in Germany by both Chapelon and Bulleid. All had faced frustration and achieved only limited success.

Now the LNER design team produced another small-scale wooden model, this time exclusively for *Mallard*. They reduced it to a one-twelfth scale and added a small plasticine funnel. Gresley gave detailed designs of his new streamliners to one of his junior assistants, Eric Bannister, with one instruction: 'solve it!'

Given the amount of energy expended on the problem already without success it seemed an impossible task for anyone, let alone a junior, but to his credit Bannister spent considerable time with Professor Dalby at his Teddington laboratory and remained optimistic.

Professor Dalby had specialised equipment but initially opted to use just this small model, together with the LNER engineering diagrams. After successive smoke tests in the wind tunnel, the model was removed and re-examined. More French chalk was added on crucial areas to simulate smoke and the model replaced. Still no change. Time after time, the wooden model was checked, withdrawn and replaced again in a special chamber. It seemed a hopeless task.

As the researchers repeated the experiment for what must have seemed like the hundredth time, they suddenly noticed a change. To their amazement, the dispersion of smoke seemed perfect. They replaced the model and tested it again and again, to make sure of their findings: each time it worked perfectly. Still scarcely able to believe their eyes, they placed the model on the laboratory's examination table. Two experts looked at the model under a magnifying lens. They noticed a small depression, no more than a thumbprint, a slightly pinched mark in the plasticine to the rear of the chimney. An assistant had accidentally touched the chimney whilst re-testing the model in the wind tunnel and must have applied slight pressure as he repositioned it. They hastily tried the model again, then tested it another three or four times. The French chalk was definitely being deflected well clear of the cab: it flew over and above the cab. It seemed unbelievable that this minor alteration was enough to make all the difference.

Suddenly, the room was full of professional people laughing, joking and hugging each other. Nearly forty years had been spent on this unusual form of testing and, amazingly, the problem had been solved by pure chance. Gresley was immediately informed by telephone: he was shocked but delighted, and wrote a memo to his chief Wedgwood confirming the success. The precise indentation was carefully noted, copied and quickly adopted within *Mallard*'s final design. (Rather surprisingly, German and French engineers continued with their old-fashioned experiments, preferring to add metallic smoke deflectors to their own prototypes.)

With *Mallard*'s launch date just weeks away, it was the best news Gresley could have possibly received. The new front-end design and chimney of *Mallard* was a brilliant adaptation and ensured the process worked effectively, dramatically improving visibility for the driver and safety standards for everyone. An ardent supporter of wind-resistance trials, Gresley believed his new A4s could not be bettered for streamlining purposes. But, as they say, the proof of the pudding was still in the eating.

Gresley could hardly wait for *Mallard* to leave Doncaster works in March 1938. In *Mallard*, he believed he had built something that was beautiful, powerful and highly functional. Every aspect of the design was right and Gresley now recognised that he had a locomotive that was slightly, but significantly, better than earlier A4s. If the LNER were to challenge the speed record again, this would be the machine that would do it.

Some colleagues reported that he was like a 'cat on hot bricks', always asking to be kept informed about developments and even initial track trials. In fact, he was contemplating one of the most difficult decisions a man in his position could make: whether to make another attack on the LMS's British speed record of 114mph.

There's no doubt the LNER was keen to have another go: the publicity and morale-boosting effects of a good run would be of huge benefit both to Gresley's company and to Britain at large. But against this desire, Gresley had to balance the risks. After fifteen highly successful years with the LNER, failure wouldn't affect his position much, particularly given the secrecy in which the proposed record attempt would to be made. But a state-of-the-art express passenger locomotive was an expensively constructed asset that was needed in regular traffic. An attempt to break the speed record would stretch the locomotive to the edge of its capacities, possibly causing it serious damage – as had happened to *Silver Fox* in 1936 – and there was always the risk of an accident. Any major failure requiring lengthy time in repairs would directly affect the company's ability to run services.

Gresley had already achieved worldwide success. At this stage in his life he was under pressure from a number of quarters: his health was poor and he was suffering from heart and respiratory problems. His physician, Sir Maurice Cassidy, had told him to take life a bit easier or else face the consequences. Gresley, stubborn as usual, would have none of it. On 19 June he celebrated his sixty-second birthday at home with family and friends. Time was becoming precious to him: he was intent on planning a golfing holiday in Scotland, where he continued a long-standing tradition of playing with several friends each year at North Berwick. Gresley had always loved his golf and had once opened the Queen's course at Gleneagles.

There were reports that LNER chairman William Whitelaw was due to retire later that month. Perhaps Gresley wanted to repay him for supporting his plans for the development of the A4 Pacifics. Whatever the case, Gresley had certainly put everything into modifying his latest engine and fully believed in her future and capabilities. At barely three months old, with her bugs ironed out but no signs of wear yet, *Mallard* was as smooth-running and as powerful as she ever would be. And she represented perhaps Gresley's last and greatest opportunity to make his mark on history. To run or not to run, that was the question, and to make the attempt he had to believe that *Mallard* was capable of beating the record; there was no question of a 'near miss' being good enough for Gresley. But he was rapidly coming towards the conclusion that it was a risk worth taking.

Imagine this bear of a man in his King's Cross office, pacing the floor for several minutes before finally sitting down and pressing a button at the side of his desk to summon his senior messenger, Mr Love. Gresley asked him to find Norman Newsome, his technical assistant for carriages and wagons, whose office was just down the corridor. Gresley knew Newsome was already in discussion with drawing-office staff over other new developments but needed his urgent advice.

A quiet, friendly man, with a reputation for applying sound engineering principles, Newsome had been born in Lincoln in 1904 and moved with his family to Doncaster when he was an infant. He joined the Great Northern Railway in 1920 as a fitter's apprentice and it was his prize-winning achievements at the local technical college that first brought him to Gresley's attention. The chief arranged for Newsome to be brought to the drawing office before he had even finished his apprenticeship and, in 1927, he was transferred to Gresley's own office at King's Cross to work with Frank Day, the technical assistant in charge of development at that time. In 1936, Day moved back to Doncaster to take charge of the central drawing office and Newsome was appointed in his place. In 1938 he was one of Gresley's most talented and trusted colleagues.

When Newsome entered his office, Gresley apparently rose from his seat and continued pacing the floor. His eyes and thoughts were clearly elsewhere; Newsome stood wondering and waiting in silence. Gresley, a keen smoker, fiddled with a box of safety matches. His pipe was well alight before he finally turned to acknowledge Newsome's presence, beckoning him to sit down. Then, through a thick cloud of smoke, he quizzed Newsome about recent brake tests on the East Coast main line. Gresley asked him to organise a special brake test a few weeks ahead. It would be a secret run for a special mission. The two men talked through all the probabilities: neither wanted a serious incident with the train but both thought the record was now a realistic proposition.

After Newsome agreed with Gresley's proposals, a further meeting was organised to iron out any other potential running problems. Then Gresley selected the men to drive and fire the engine, both hand-picked to give the LNER the best possible chance of taking the record.

Joe Duddington, who always wore his cloth cap back to front in traditional racing style, was a respected and experienced driver, capable of pushing the engine hard. He had nursed *Mallard* from the moment the locomotive left the works; he referred to her as his own property and took a particular pride in her right from the start. Born on 8 August 1876, he had entered the service of GNR at the age of eighteen in March 1895, first working as an engine cleaner at Doncaster works. In March 1898, he was 'passed' for firing duties and gained considerable experience on the footplate. At the end of this period, Duddington was promoted to spare driver, becoming eligible for shunting engine and relieving duties. He reached the stage of mainline driver in March 1913 and subsequently worked all classes of trains running between Leeds, York and King's Cross, and the Nottingham and Lincolnshire districts. Over the next twenty-five years he gained a wide variety of experience on the footplate during the rapid advances in locomotive design under the regimes of Stirling, Ivatt and Gresley. And he had an extraordinary knowledge of the first Ivatt Atlantics and A4 Pacifics.

Duddington had had many exciting moments during his career as a driver: on one occasion, an embankment collapsed while his parcels train was passing over it and, although the engine kept to the rails, several vans at the rear were derailed and rolled down the embankment. Another incident took place whilst he was driving an important passenger express train. At high speed and without any warning, the inside connecting rod broke into several pieces. Incredibly, there were no casualties in either incident.

The choice of Duddington to drive the engine is in complete contrast to current practice – how many men over fifty would be given the chance to break speed records today? But Gresley had studied his records and knew his man's superb capabilities. He also knew that in Tommy Bray he had an excellent fireman. With tattoos covering his arms, Bray had been with *Mallard* for as long as Duddington had, and could work a Pacific to the limit. They were the ideal partnership.

Towards the end of June 1938, Duddington and Bray received a message via Gresley's King's Cross office: they were needed for a special mission, the details to be kept absolutely secret. There had been speculation for weeks that something special was on the cards. The LNER press office had been remarkably subdued over developments and Gresley's own personal staff remained tight-lipped. All that was publicly known was that Norman Newsome had been put in charge of organising a special brake test.

After discussions with Gresley, the next scheduled test date was agreed for Sunday 3 July. Newsome liaised with all the relevant departments and was responsible for all the preparations. The train would include three twin sets from the Coronation stock, together with the dynamometer car. Gresley insisted that the locomotive would be A4 class No. 4468, *Mallard* and her Doncaster crew, instead of the usual King's Cross team.

The dynamometer car – the vehicle which recorded train performance - was a luxury coach on its own. It was also a practical working vehicle and could accommodate up to six or seven crew members, each measuring or recording vital information. It was constructed of beautiful light-brown teak with the front part of its outer body forming a convex shape, rather like the polished wooden boards of an upturned rowing boat – standard for Great Northern Railway and, later, LNER carriages. The interior was exquisitely designed with luxurious padded seats, similar teak décor and a dazzling mass of brass and glass instrumentation. The coach even had a decorative ceramic patterned toilet and wash-room, fold-back chairs, and limited catering facilities, with a small stove.

Dynamometer No. 902502 had been built in 1906 by the North Eastern Railway and used extensively by them and later by the London & North Eastern Railway following the 1923 grouping. The data obtained by cars such as this one were later used to improve design and prepare and modify train schedules. The equipment measured several variables and, using calculation, a number of other vital statistics could be obtained. A calibrated, flangeless wheel, which could be raised and lowered as necessary, measured the distance travelled. In addition, a very large, near frictionless leaf spring connected to the carriage draw-hook measured force or drawbar pull. Pens on a roll of paper, known as the dynamometer roll, recorded all the information. Dynamometer No. 902502 is now preserved in original condition at the National Railway Museum in York.

These, then, were the ingredients needed for success.

The standard brake tests were normally carried out first on suburban trains and on one of the 'Coronation' high-speed trains. They worked on Sundays when the rolling stock was not required for passenger service, and each Monday after the tests Gresley was informed of the results. The brake trials at this time were primarily designed to work locomotives and stock with the Westinghouse Brake Company to test the new QSA vacuum brake system but on this occasion Gresley wanted to use the return leg to give *Mallard* her head of steam. The train was scheduled to begin duties from Wood Green waterworks sidings on the outskirts of London to Barkston, a few miles north of Grantham. It was to depart shortly before noon, and at Barkston, the engine and dynamometer car would be turned on a triangle of lines to face south.

Newsome later recalled:

It was following one of these tests after the results had been discussed that Gresley enquired when the next test was to take place. I told him that we were proposing to go again on July 3rd. He then said he intended to attempt to beat the record of 114mph achieved by the LMS and we discussed the formation of the train.

It was agreed that the dynamometer car would be used and a set of Coronation coaches would be reduced by one articulated unit, making seven coaches in all. I was informed that instead of the usual streamlined locomotive which had been employed in the brake tests, *Mallard* was to be used with a Doncaster crew – rather than the usual London crew and locomotive.

All this meant that as a brake test the run would not be comparable with what we had previously done. Nevertheless, arrangements were put in hand for brake tests to be staged between London and Peterborough as usual. However, the train would go on to Barkston, where the engine and dynamometer car would be placed at the London end of the train.

As usual in our brake tests we had railway representatives from the Westinghouse Brake Company. They were not informed of what was to take place but when they saw that the train formation was different from usual, they started asking questions.

In our normal brake tests inspector Sam Jenkins was in charge of the locomotive, and I was responsible for the tests on the train. But on this occasion Mr Douglass Edge, who was Gresley's personal assistant, and my chief, was in charge on the train; and Bernard Adkinson of the locomotive running department was in charge of the locomotive and its crew.

Denis Carling, an LNER test inspector, was also involved on the brake tests. Late in June, Tom Robson, chief test inspector of LNER, informed his dynamometer car staff that the car would be needed for some brake trials. The car travelled up from Darlington on Saturday 2 July, and on the same day *Mallard* arrived at King's Cross top shed.

Gresley later spoke with the footplate crew at top sheds, giving instructions to his deputy, Douglass Edge, and telling him what was expected. During the weeks leading up the brake tests, he had arranged with Dandridge in publicity to have a number of static and action shots of *Mallard* available for distribution – just in case.

LNER test inspector Denis Carling was a member of the dynamometer car staff during *Mallard*'s test run. At the sheds he had installed a special intercom between *Mallard*'s cab and the car as soon as she arrived from Darlington. He also explained some of the preparatory work that day:

> I was test inspector to Christopher Jarvis and Percy Dobson. Knowing that high speeds would be involved and particular accuracy of measurement required, we changed the gears driving the recording paper to give it a speed of two feet per mile in place of the usual one foot and checked the car's braking system and running gear – especially the lubrication.
>
> Changing the paper speed would provide greater accuracy in measuring both the speed and distance. We did not need to record the action of actual train brakes as this was being done by the staff from Westinghouse. Inspector Sam Jenkins, of the locomotive running department, was to be on the footplate and would use the intercom to inform the test inspector at the dynamometer car table of the locomotive working so that it could be noted on the record.
>
> The brake trials took place as usual at a number of suitable locations on the 'down' journey from speeds of between 90mph and 100mph, the stopping distances being subsequently measured from the dynamometer car record.

Max Hoather, from the Westinghouse team, also later remembered some of the details of the test run:

> The object of the brake trials was to improve upon the performance of the brake system in order to reduce the stopping distance of the new streamline trains.
>
> It was necessary to work these trains on a double-block system, which interfered with the smooth running of the main line traffic. In response to Gresley's request, we developed a

modification of the standard vacuum brake system with a quick acting (QSA) valve – one of which was attached to the brake cylinders. Because a higher brake force than usual was needed for the streamline trains, cylinders with a twenty-four diameter were employed.

Everything was in place. Now only time would tell if Gresley's locomotive was capable of entering the history books.

Chapter Eleven
The Day of Reckoning

n 3 July 1938, *Mallard* arrived for her big day in perfect working order. She was dead on time and looked as magnificent as any locomotive ever had. Her impressive streamlined body, cab and valances appeared in a superb garter-blue livery. Her smokebox was jet black with delicate lines taken around the sides in a narrow parabolic curve, and her enormous powerful driving wheels were painted in a rich Coronation red. She carried new-style brass- and chromium-plated nameplates on both sides of her front boiler. They sparkled, reflecting the hard work put in the day before at King's Cross shed by the engine cleaners to make her presentable for special duties.

As she pulled into the sidings at Wood Green waterworks, there was surely an intake of breath from members gathered at the trackside. The locomotive's polished bodywork and silver buffers shimmered in the morning sunshine. The luxury coaches, too, appeared in almost identical garter blue below the waistline, with a slightly lighter Marlborough blue above. Behind *Mallard* was the equally magnificent, teak-panelled dynamometer car No. 902502, coupled to three twin-sets of luxury carriages from the 'Coronation' Pullman express.

All was set for Gresley's finest hour – but he wasn't on the train that day. His deteriorating health meant he remained at home. He knew his personal appearance would attract attention and he did not want to risk the wrath of his physician. One wonders whether, if he had known what was going to happen, he'd have ignored his doctor's orders. In his place on the train was his personal assistant, Douglass Edge, together with Norman

Newsome and Bernard Adkinson from the locomotive running department, among others. Also present was Eric Bannister, who had helped Professor Dalby solve the A4 chimney problem; perhaps his inclusion in the party was Gresley's idea of a reward or maybe Bannister himself wanted to gain valuable experience.

At this stage, only a select handful knew the real purpose of the test run, which was not revealed to the crew until just before the train left Wood Green. The orders were explicit: this was to be an attack on the LMS's British record of 114mph. The record attempt was most definitely on. It had everything going for it: the right crew, the right locomotive and, crucially, the right stretch of track.

The plan was that the train would head for a place in Lincolnshire called Barkston. Situated just a few miles north of Grantham where the branch to Sleaford and Boston left the main line, Barkston had little to recommend it to sightseers – but it did have a triangle of lines where whole trains could be turned. It was often used as a convenient turning point for locomotives on test runs after repairs at Doncaster. Critically, departing south from Barkston would give the locomotive a good run up to Stoke Bank, where the record was to be attempted.

Shortly before departure from London, Norman Newsome smiled and looked at his clipboard. He noticed that several officials from the Westinghouse Company seemed unexpectedly rattled at the appearance of the dynamometer car, which was generally only used for high-speed testing. Not everyone was in on the secret.

The party were told the train would depart from Wood Green at 11.46 a.m. with stops en route at Welwyn Garden City, Stevenage, Langford Bridge, Holme, Peterborough and Barkston. The brake tests were to take place on the northbound journey under the supervision of the Westinghouse officials. The train was scheduled to arrive at Barkston shortly before 3 p.m.

Despite the nerves he must have been feeling that day, New-some seemed perfectly relaxed. He watched as one of his col-leagues checked off the staff list and the names of those travelling, including the driver, Joe Duddington, fireman Bray and a railway guard, who later admitted he was more used to freight trains than brake tests. Should the riding become rough at the unprecedented speeds to be attempted, his experience on bucking brake vans would hold him in good stead. The Westing-house team consisted of Mr Le Clair as the senior member, A.G. Brackenbury, Max Hoather and P.T.W. Remnant. Each member was given a special ticket for insurance and safety reasons – an ominous sign.

Mallard's planned speed was such that it was essential to find clear track for the run to take place. The train would be running so fast that the normal gaps between signals, designed to allow a train to stop safely from its top speed, were far too short. This meant the signalmen from Grantham to King's Cross would have to give *Mallard* two signals for her to have a chance of stopping in time. In the normal course of things, this would have been impossible, but in that era the Sabbath was observed far more closely than it is today, and the reduced number of services run-ning meant that it was not too difficult to find a space.

As departure time approached, the tension started to mount as everyone realised the importance of the mission they were embarking on. Inspector Jenkins climbed up to the cab and shook hands with the footplate crew, then tested the equipment and intercom to the dynamometer car. On the train, there was an atmosphere of nervous excitement. Normally the 'Coronation' express was packed with genuine passengers attended by uni-formed assistants. This time, however, the train was eerily empty, with just a handful of seats taken and people scattered throughout the train. Because of the anticipated speeds, no paying passengers were allowed on, and the guard had to make a long lonely walk down the train before settling into his rear compartment. Most of those travelling were in the dynamometer car at the front of the express.

Duddington gave *Mallard* a couple of loud toots on her chime whistle and at precisely 11.46 a.m. the signal lifted, and the guard, who was half hanging out of his rear window, gave three short, sharp blows on his whistle, before waving his flag furiously towards the driver. With a slight jerking movement and a great surge of pure white steam from the cylinder drain cocks, the train edged slowly forward. It clattered across the points and on to the main line and quickly began to gather pace. The officials in the dynamometer car looked anxiously at each other, trying to keep themselves busy but no doubt wondering if the train was about to make a journey into history.

The immaculate *Mallard* soon made steady progress towards Potters Bar, whizzing through the lush green railway cuttings like a huge snake, twisting and writhing with the beat of the tracks and the purpose of her mission. A swath of pure white smoke, like a long tail of cotton wool, trailed along the tops of the roofs of her adjacent dynamometer car and three Coronation carriage twin sets.

Initially, the day followed the pattern of a normal brake test. Brake trials took place as usual at a number of suitable locations on the northbound journey at speeds of between 90mph and 100mph, the stopping distances being subsequently measured from the dynamometer car record. In the dynamometer car, the LNER officials were hastily adding the final touches to their own work schedules. At the tip-up seat on the offside bow was Denis Carling, the LNER test inspector. On the opposite side was Percy Dobson. Gresley's deputy Douglass Edge was at the main desk in the centre of the car, accompanied by Bernard Adkinson and Chris Jarvis. Other staff members had various duties and kept coming in and out of the test car from different compartments. Norman Newsome seemed well settled in first class, with Leslie

Nicholson, Richard Stubley, Eric Bannister and G.H. Taylor reporting for additional duties.

On the footplate were Duddington, Bray and inspector Jenkins. Regular contact and updates were relayed back and forth from the dynamometer car to the footplate by intercom and the timings were checked and agreed.

'Wood Green, 11.46 a.m. departure,' was the first time shouted out and recorded. The train noticeably gathered speed. Soon other timings were shouted across the car. 'Potters Bar 11.59 a.m. passed; Hatfield 12.03 passed.' The train stopped briefly at Welwyn Garden City at 12.06, and then departed a minute later. The brake tests continued and again details were shouted out and recorded as necessary amidst a number of pre-arranged stops and starts.

And so *Mallard* headed north, the timings recording her progress. 'Stevenage arrive 12.18, then depart 12.23. Hitchin passed at 12.27, Langford Bridge arrived 12.33, then departed 12.35, Sandy passed 12.45, Everton passed 1.10 p.m., Huntingdon passed 1.25, Holme arrived 1.35, then departed 1.36.' A few noses must have been pressed to the carriage windows as they rattled through, eyes following the station name signs as they disappeared into a blur.

When the train arrived at Peterborough at precisely 1.46 p.m., the dynamometer crew took a few moments to collect their thoughts. They knew that within a couple of hours, *Mallard* and her special train would be back there, with or without the record. Surely hearts were starting to beat faster, pulses beginning to race and nerves were tingling. Some less anxious members took the opportunity to stretch their legs on the platform.

Eventually, twenty-six minutes later, everyone shuffled back inside, the guard blew his whistle, doors were slammed and the train left. By the time they passed slowly through Grantham at 2.41 p.m., the tension was at near breaking point. This would be the crucial starting point for the build-up of steam on the high-speed run. They arrived at Barkston at 2.49 p.m. where the train prepared to move across into a siding. As Denis Carling later reported, 'The "down" journey ended at Barkston where the locomotive and dynamometer car were turned on the triangle and the train parked clear of the main line whilst we ate the packed lunches provided. Norman Newsome got a key to the kitchen of the dining car and got the tea boiler working to assuage our thirst.' A late lunch and a cup of tea – it was a typically, wonderfully British preparation for an attempt to make history.

There was a little while before departure, and most people remained sitting in the restaurant car. As the time approached, nerves started to tingle and anxiety returned again: like parachutists approaching the drop zone, few spoke, preferring to smile or acknowledge their companions silently. During the wait at Barkston, Sam Jenkins and Eric Bannister, who was Bert Spencer's draughtsman, thoroughly doused the middle big end with super-heater oil as a precaution against overheating. The men also used another unusual tactic to avoid overheating: the addition of a stink bomb, inserted within the mechanical workings near the middle big end. A simple device which gave off strong-smelling fumes if the temperature got too high, the stink bomb effectively acted as an early-warning system, thus preventing undue damage.

After lunch, Jenkins then made up *Mallard*'s fire with Tommy Bray and re-tested the intercom and equipment with the footplate crew in readiness for the high-speed run. Preparing the fire was crucial – it must be really hot in order to generate the vast quantities of steam needed to break the British record. Officials did a quick roll call and made sure everyone was on board and seated exactly where they were supposed to be for recording purposes. The atmosphere must have been fraught – a mixture of excitement, apprehension and fear. All would have to give their fullest concentration for the next half-hour or so.

Just before departure, Douglass Edge suddenly called the

Westinghouse team together. He addressed senior member Mr Le Clair, telling him what was about to happen, and asked if anyone wanted to take a taxi back to Peterborough instead of risking a fast run. Unanimously, all agreed to stay and, with Cheshire cat-like grins on their faces, hastily took their seats in the first class section of the Coronation coaches. It was time.

Mallard gave a couple of hoots in readiness and there was the sound of the guard's whistle blowing. The train shuffled forward slightly then slowly pulled away and back on to the main line. The locomotive left Barkston South junction at exactly 4.15 p.m. In the first class section tea was served to members, including the Westinghouse team: Peterborough was now just over half an hour away.

Once again, the dynamometer car became a hive of activity. Riding inside the car were Douglass Edge, who was in charge of proceedings; Percy Dobson from Doncaster works, who sat at the main desk with the telephone microphone relaying information to and from the driver's cab; and Denis Carling, who sat on a tip seat using a bell push to mark on the record any mile posts, gradient boards and bridges which would locate the train at any one time. Mr Adkinson and Christopher Jarvis were also in the car, and P.T.W. Remnant of the Westinghouse contingent took the opportunity to join them there.

The journey started badly at Grantham station. Remnant recalled, 'Platelayers were doing some Sunday maintenance work on the track and there were several speed restrictions. Their upturned faces registered surprise as we passed. There were some wry smiles as the speed fell back to 18mph.'

Despite this slack, and the big fire he undoubtedly built up, fireman Bray shovelled coal furiously – he knew that when speed got really high, it would be burning up almost as fast as he hurled it in to the firebox.

Denis Carling later recalled:

The 'up' journey began normally but instead of passing Grantham at the usual 60–70mph for a non-stop express, we had to slow down for a temporary speed restriction to just 15mph because of work on the track. Driver Duddington observed the restriction exactly and we passed the middle of the station at 24mph and then *Mallard* was worked very hard up the bank so as to pass the summit as fast as possible.

Past the onerous restriction, the recording paper started to move and it was not long before Duddington had got *Mallard* up to 65mph – she was starting to take wing, her boiler at full pressure. In the cab, Duddington was in his element: 'I accelerated up the bank to Stoke summit and passed Stoke box at 85. Once over the top, I gave *Mallard* her head and she just jumped to it like a live thing.'

There was excitement in the dynamometer car too; Remnant wrote in his account, 'As we entered Stoke Tunnel, there was a slight delay before the guard switched on the lights, and the passengers were treated to a thrilling display as the whole car was lit up by a torrent of red-hot cinders streaming back on both sides from the locomotive's twin chimneys.'

The fireman's workload increased: if there were any small lumps of coal, they may not even have made contact with the fire, being sucked through the boiler tubes and out through the chimney. With a lively locomotive riding well, but unavoidably vibrating, getting the coal through the firehole at all needed an expert. As speed continued to rise, Bray was proving why he had been chosen for the job, and justifying every penny of his wages.

Inside the dynamometer car, people started to smile: it was looking good. The train had passed Stoke summit at about 6mph faster than *Silver Fox* when the previous LNER record of 113mph was set. *Mallard* then accelerated the train down the bank, gathering speed nearly twice as fast as *Silver Fox* had done with a train only some thirty tons heavier. According to Carling, this was 'due partly to *Silver Fox* not having been let out until some way further down the bank and partly to the benefit of *Mallard*'s Kylchap exhaust system, specially designed by André Chapelon at Sir Nigel's request'.

Measurements were now being taken with tight-lipped concentration as the train accelerated down the bank – drawbar horsepower, 1,200 – cut-off, 40%. If the record was going to fall, it would happen soon. Duddington later reported: 'After three miles the speedometer in my cab showed 107 miles an hour, then 108, 109, 110 – getting near *Silver Fox*'s record of 113. I thought, I wonder if I can get past that, well we'll try and before I knew it, the needle was at 116 and we'd got the record.'

Duddington pushed *Mallard* still harder, perhaps lengthening the cut-off as far as he could to get every last breath of steam from the boiler into her three voracious cylinders. In the dynamometer car, the pointer of the speedometer crept up to 120: the LMS record was beaten, but could *Mallard* beat the Germans? She only had a brief period to make her mark; when she got to the curves at Essendine, she would have to slow down.

There were smiles all round but still an air of great expectancy. Through a cutting, swaying, rocking, 120, then off the end of the speedometer scale, 123 perhaps? They were over the 120 all right but the crew still believed there was more to come. There was massive excitement in the train, and when the recorder showed 122mph for a mile and a half the tension was at fever pitch. In the cab, Duddington and Bray were giving it their all: 'Go on girl, I thought, we can do better than this. I nursed her and shot through Little Bytham at 123 . . .'

It must have been around this time that Bray flung the last, fateful shovelful of coal into *Mallard*'s blazing furnace. After a couple of seconds, it added its heat to the fire, the water boiled a little more furiously, the steam went to the cylinders at a slightly higher pressure, and, critically, the wheels went round that little bit faster. Duddington was still thrashing *Mallard*: in the next one and a quarter miles, the needle crept up further, 123.5, 124, 125 ... For a quarter of a mile, the crew in the dynamometer car held their breaths as the train reached 126 miles per hour. The British – and the German records – had been beaten by a team and a machine at the very top of their form.

Was there more? Could Mallard hit 130mph as Gresley believed she could? The men in the dynamometer car knew Essendine was coming up: should they let Duddington carry on? Percy Dobson reported the speeds to Douglass Edge: 'Well, Mr Edge, we're over the 120 all right but I should think he still has something in hand. Shall I let him carry on?' Essendine tunnel was approaching at unprecedented speed, and nobody wanted the adventure to end in disaster. Edge made the painful decision to ease up and, reluctantly, Dobson gave the word via the telephone link.

The drawbar pull diagram broke its steady rise and speed started to fall. By then, as the train was nearing the junctions at Essendine, steam was shut off and the brakes applied. Even so, it passed the station at about 108mph – way above the nominal 90mph restriction.

Mallard was rocking slightly from side to side but as she came to the left-hand curve approaching Essendine station, she heeled to an appreciable angle and Denis Carling wondered if she might heel over even more the other way when they reached the right-hand curve beyond the station. Suddenly, things weren't so much fun. As Carling recalled, 'We ran quite smoothly through the curves, points, crossings, bad patch and all but soon afterwards a distinctive odour told us that Mallard's big end was hot enough to burst the stink bomb in the hollow crank pin.'

Instead of an easy run to a triumphant welcome at King's Cross, *Mallard* would have to slow down and limp to Peterborough; there was no way she could make London without completely wrecking herself. The blue streak's big day was over – but she had done all that was asked of her and more.

In the dynamometer car, there were handshakes and smiles all round, then heads started popping up out of windows. These men had watched the drama played out not in the blurring of the countryside but in the wavering of a pen on a chart. But of all the men on the train these knew the news first: their train would be in the record books.

Speed started to fall as *Mallard* inched towards Peterborough, now lame following her overheated big end. An examination when she stopped at Peterborough confirmed that the white metal had melted and the locomotive would have to come off the train. Carling remembered, 'We got our equipment off in record time before the Peterborough pilot came on to take the train on to London.' Remnant was so excited that he rushed to the footplate to congratulate the crew; he recalled, 'Fitters were soon swarming all over *Mallard*. The doors in the streamlined casing were opened. The centre big end had gone all right and *Mallard* was replaced by an old Ivatt Atlantic.'

There was just one thing left to do. Douglass Edge rang up Sir Nigel Gresley at his home at Watton-at-Stone and told him what had happened. Gresley's reaction is unrecorded, but one imagines him pacing his living room anxiously waiting for the telephone call to give him the good (or the bad) news. When the phone rang and Gresley went to answer it, he must have paused while he heard the news, and then what? He wasn't a man to jump for joy, but surely a smile must have spread across his face: *Mallard* had done it.

It was only after the train had reached King's Cross that the dynamometer car records could be examined and the record speed confirmed. As Carling explained, 'A preliminary examination of the record showed that 124.5mph had been reached for 10 seconds and later that 125mph had been attained for 5 seconds. Some time later 126mph was finally established, only for one second, or about 60 yards.'

Mallard had handsomely beaten the claimed LMS record of 114mph and just exceeded the 124.5mph of the Deutsche Reichsbahn 05, 4-6-4. Even more important for railwaymen was that 120mph had been exceeded for over three miles – and averaged for over five. Had the train passed Grantham at about 70mph instead of 15–24mph, she could have passed Stoke summit at up to 10mph faster, depending on how Duddington might have worked the engine: nobody will ever know just what her top speed could have been.

At 6.27 p.m. the train arrived at King's Cross to meet the press, who had already been alerted, and who were taken to the dynamometer car and shown the charts. Eric Bannister, the junior member of the team, had earlier been briefed by Gresley and officials. He had arranged for the press office to have some photographs of *Mallard*, and when the train arrived back in London, he dropped off the car by the footbridge and sprinted to his office next to Platform 10 to collect the pictures. The Atlantic which had taken over the train at Peterborough was uncoupled and removed so quickly that it was passing under the bridge just as Bannister returned. Weary but happy, the passengers alighted. With superb understatement, one commented: 'A very interesting and exciting day was had by all of us who took part.'

In an interview with the BBC in 1944, Duddington spoke of his and Bray's efforts, with pride but without hyperbole. His was a characteristic modesty: without their bravery, skill and sweat, this fantastic record could not have happened. Without Duddington's superb judgement about what level of rough riding constituted a danger, and Bray's ability to fling the coal through the dinner-plate-sized firehole on an increasingly shaking footplate, all of *Mallard*'s superb design would have been for naught.

In retrospect, the irritating speed restriction at Grantham amplifies *Mallard*'s tremendous achievement. In just twenty-six minutes from passing Grantham to arriving at Peterborough, *Mallard* had run herself ragged and into the record books to achieve a brilliant and unbeaten result of 126mph. It wasn't quite the smooth ride some claimed; notes at the library in the National Railway Museum at York record, 'The train shook so violently that crockery smashed to the floor, and given the chance the guard would have happily got off.' The guard was normally a goods guard and unused to high speeds but in his records he said he thought the Coronation set rode better at 120mph than a guard's van at 20mph. There were also claims that Little Bytham station, in the midst of the speed route, had some windows broken and the platform was scattered with hot ashes as she roared through at more than 120mph.

LNER enthusiast Leslie Burley later remarked: 'When I saw the train return through New Barnet, with Atlantic, No. 3290, still with four-column GN safety valves, I was certain A4, No. 4468, *Mallard* had been driven hard. The "up" train was about on time although it would not have made the brake stops. Word soon came down the line to the signal boxes from control of the remarkable achievement.'

For Gresley, it was the ultimate vindication of his decision to go for the attempt, and proof of the brilliance of *Mallard*'s design. And, despite losing his British record, Gresley's long-time rival and friend, William Stanier, CME of LMS, was one of the first to congratulate him, writing generously:

My Dear Gresley,

What a magnificent effort. Sincerest congratulations on the fine performance of *Mallard* yesterday. I shall be very interested in seeing the details of the run and particulars of the engine working at some future time, yours very sincerely,

W.A. Stanier.

By the time *Mallard*'s footplate crew sat down for their supper on 3 July, her 126mph (at that time 125mph) record was headline news around the world. Bulletins were issued by the BBC and confirmation soon reached testing sites in Germany, France and the United States, where top railway engineers probably scratched their heads in frustration and admiration – no doubt feeling a little prick of jealousy.

Christened the 'Blue Streak' by an admiring media, Gresley's magnificent flying machine had achieved a speed never before, or since, verifiably reached by a steam locomotive. Joe Duddington and Tommy Bray had their names written into the record books forever; their lives would never be quite the same again. Overnight, the pair became national celebrities. Their faces soon appeared in the *Daily Express*, which showed Duddington in his trademark cloth cap – which he had characteristically worn back to front for the record run – receiving a kiss of greeting from his daughter Marjorie. The article accompanying the photograph revealed that although he could handle a massive steam locomotive travelling at 125mph he was too nervous to get behind the wheel of a car. Tommy Bray, too, revelled in the limelight for a few days, exposing his colourful and highly tattooed arms in photographs. He described them as a picture gallery and said that in years to come he, too, wanted to become an engine driver.

Both men remained philosophical about the record: while they knew it was a tremendous achievement, they considered it just part of their job. As far as Duddington was concerned, he had simply been told to go 'flat out, and give *Mallard* her head', and that was exactly what he did. He admitted to nursing her along at times, even caressing *Mallard* with soft words, but he believed in her capabilities. To his dying day, Duddington reckoned that *Mallard* was 'the best engine ever built – and which ever will be built'. He described her as a 'masterpiece', adding, 'They don't build them like her any more.' In years to come the only tinge of regret he felt concerned the delay at Grantham; without that he believed she could have reached 130mph.

The very next day after their triumph Duddington and Bray were on the footplate of another passenger express running from Doncaster to King's Cross. Duddington was later in charge of the regulator for a few other memorable steam trips, but only a few years after *Mallard*'s record-breaking run, he retired, and died in 1948. Tommy Bray achieved his ambition to become a driver and continued driving for several more years before his death. The two men stayed friends throughout their lives.

The day after the run, newspapers throughout the country gave a detailed account of *Mallard*'s triumph but the story failed to hog the headlines since other world events were dominating the news. Although almost every newspaper in Britain carried some front-page news about the record, most led on events in the Spanish Civil War, where heavy bombing raids on Barcelona were failing to weaken morale. Other papers ran with news of further threats from the Nazis and corruption in Austria.

Some foreign papers claimed that Gresley had said at the time: '*Mallard*'s achievement was tremendous as a publicity stunt – and a highly successful one – but the A4s can do very little that an A3 can't, but look more spectacular doing it.' Perhaps the most entertaining response to *Mallard*'s run, however, came from Germany, where the press and Third Reich officials were remarkably quiet following her remarkable performance. Later, they claimed the record had only been achieved due to the falling gradient and challenged whether it had reached 125mph for any great length of time. Furthermore, they claimed Gresley could afford to risk *Mallard* as she was just one of about fifty Pacifics. The number of locomotives in the fleet didn't stop the Germans hitting 124.5mph, however, so this seems a somewhat flawed argument to say the least.

The *Stamford Mercury*, the region's local paper, visited the railway station and signal box nearest to the place where *Mallard* gained the record. The newspaper's headline naturally focused on local pride: 'Fastest rail track in England – British record smashed near Little Bytham. First two-mile a minute train.' The village of Little Bytham had in fact been an important railway centre during the nineteenth century, where passengers and freight using local lines could also find connections to other parts of the country. The area possessed vast clay deposits used for Roman pottery. In the nineteenth century, the bricks and pantiles it produced won national acclaim for their fine quality and were used in the construction of the railway viaduct that still dominates the village.

Although the region is no longer so important, it remains notable because it nestles beneath a grand Victorian viaduct that still carries the main London to Scotland East Coast line. More than four decades after *Mallard* won the record, a sixteenth-century hostelry in Little Bytham's high street known originally as the Green Man changed its name to Mallard, both to commemorate the locomotive's triumph and to acknowledge the role of railways in the area. The viaduct that once witnessed the feats of the steam expresses is still in operation, used mainly by high-speed diesel and electric trains, but the odd steam-hauled charter train runs past too, at up to 75mph.

Despite the acclaim Gresley and his team deservedly received, there was some doubt about whether *Mallard* had achieved 125 or 126mph. Gresley was told 125 at first and it seems to have been some time later before the final figure was confirmed. For his part, Gresley himself never really accepted 126mph. Even so, there was sufficient evidence to claim the record and all facts were later supported by official documentary evidence.

The Mechanical Engineer Design Testing and Performance Section at Darlington later analysed *Mallard*'s performance and the results were published from the chief mechanical engineer's department at King's Cross. In extracts from their reports, they confirm:

> It was always the practice to calculate speeds on average basis because they had to be measured up from the record and calculated from time and distance. By taking a time interval to give a

longer distance, the inaccuracies are a smaller percentage.

On the high-speed run, the paper was moving through at the rate of two feet to a mile. At this high paper speed, a time interval of five seconds was measured for average speed and the speeds shown on the record are, therefore, average speeds over 5 seconds. Previous consideration has always accepted that it was a peak speed during the 5-second period of 125mph.

An assessment has now been made by measuring the average speed over 1-second intervals and an accurate curve drawn to show the peak of 126mph at about 90 miles, 220 yards from London.

The chart shows that during *Mallard*'s performance, she achieved 126.1mph over a distance of 61.6 yards for a measurement on record at 2ft to a mile, inches of 0.840. *Mallard* exceeded 120mph between 92.75 and 89.75 mile posts and an average speed between 94 and 89-mile posts of 120.4mph.

Cecil J. Allen, one of the most highly respected recorders for speed trials, later published an official report of the journey in a railway magazine. He confirmed that the train had consisted of three of the Coronation twin sets, plus the dynamometer car, coming to seven vehicles in all, weighing 240 tons. He added: '*Mallard* had travelled faster, not only than the LMS Corporation, but also than all other steam locomotives in the world, whose high-speed performances, properly authenticated by a sequence of passing times, are on record.'

Debate about the *Mallard* speed record continued, with test inspector Denis Carling suggesting that, size for size, the British and German locomotive designs were well matched.

A point about the heated big end. I believe that this was due to shutting off steam at 120mph. The force required to stop the motion of the piston, crosshead and part of the connecting rod at each end of the stroke is very large; normally with steam on part of this force comes the compression of the steam still in the cylinder, but with steam off the force all has to come from the crank pin, thus overloading the bearing.

This opinion is confirmed because at least three similar hot bearings on the German 05s were attributed by their designer to the same cause. Had the maximum speed with *Mallard* been attained sooner, and steam shut off gradually there would probably have been no overheating at all.

In comparing the top speeds of the British A4 and the German 05 several points need to be considered. Firstly, the 05 class of only three locomotives were specially designed for high-speed between Berlin and Hamburg; whereas the A4 was a class of general service express locomotives for which three high-speed trains were only a small, if important part of their duties.

The 05's speed was maintained for a much greater distance and on a smaller falling gradient but with a mightier train although it was an appreciably larger locomotive.

Records apart, both classes gave very good reliable service though both had their troubles on occasion. It seems remarkable, not that one might be slightly superior to the other, but that two locomotives of different origin should be so nearly equal.

Incredibly, the debate with German rail enthusiasts continues even to this day, more than six decades after the event. The Third Reich-backed 05.002 steam locomotive achieved 124.5mph with a 197-tonne load. It reached 110mph on at least five occasions, 115mph four times and 120mph twice. *Mallard* certainly touched 126.1mph for just over sixty yards. She also travelled at over 120mph for more than three miles, and averaged her top speed for more than five miles. She also matched the German record at exactly 124.5mph for 10 seconds before increasing to 126mph, while hauling 240 tons, substantially more than her German rival. It seems impossible to doubt that her performance was superior.

On 12 July, nine days after her epic performance, *Mallard* once again appeared in public, when she came up on the 1.47 p.m. arrival, and returned from King's Cross on the 4 p.m. Further high-speed runs were already being anticipated, perhaps in 1939.

This time, 130mph (and perhaps faster) was being seriously considered by the LNER – perhaps Joe Duddington hoped he might finally get his chance to see just how fast *Mallard* could go. However, it was not to be. Rapidly increasing political tensions meant it was clear that there would be a war, and one in which the railways would play a major part. For the moment, speed attempts would have to go by the wayside.

Chapter Twelve
After the Record

Not long after the breaking of the record, in September 1938, Prime Minister Neville Chamberlain acceded to Hitler's demands to occupy the Sudetenland. But from now on war was inevitable. On 1 September 1939 Hitler invaded Poland and the British government, anticipating bombing raids, began to evacuate children from the major cities. Trains were specially chartered for evacuees, and among them were the last streamlined services to run until after the war.

When the war began on 3 September, freight took preference on main lines and blackout conditions prevailed throughout the country. High-speed passenger services were no longer considered a priority and the powerful A4 class was expensive to run and maintain. As a result, many were put into storage at the outset of hostilities, including *Mallard*, though fortunately she only remained locked away for a week from 31 October to 6 November 1939. *Mallard* had her valances covering the wheels removed to ease servicing and create easier access for oiling. On 15 June 1942, *Mallard* registered 68,020 miles since her last service and was repainted in her jet blackout livery, which she retained until nationalisation in January 1948. In October 1943, she transferred to Grantham depot from Doncaster.

Like many similar members of her class, she suffered from lack of regular maintenance and equipment. It was a problem that beset many other A4s that kept running throughout the war and led to a host of mechanical problems for the three-cylinder engines. Other trains also sustained indignities. The memorable chime whistles were removed from all the class and destroyed in 1942 because the emergency government thought the whistle could cause confusion if the public mistook it for an air-raid signal. New (and popular) chime whistles were refitted again after the war. A few locomotives became casualties: A4 Pacific, No. 4469, *Sir Ralph Wedgwood*, was destroyed by the Luftwaffe during an air raid on York on 29 April 1942. The locomotive was later scrapped but the tender retained. One wonders if the Reichsbahn officials had kept the LNER documents specifying the service details following their request for an estimate with the *Flying Hamburger* service in 1933. Or did they pass them on to the Luftwaffe?

Sir Nigel Gresley himself was another casualty of the war. Shortly after *Mallard*'s triumph his health began to deteriorate and chronic bronchitis set in. He had increasing problems walking and soon his heart began to fail. He managed a final holiday in Devon with his daughter, Vi, and even attended the unveiling of his final steam locomotive, *Bantam Cock*, and his first electric engine, No. 6701, at York on 19 February 1941. But because of worsening health he had to turn down invitations to a number of other ceremonies, including one to the launch of his friend Oliver Bulleid's latest locomotive, the *Merchant Navy* Pacific.

Gresley died at his home at Watton-on-Stone in the presence of his son, Roger, on 5 April 1941. He was only sixty-four. A few days later, he was buried next to his wife, underneath the Boscobel oak tree in the family graveyard at Netherseale. He was the last member of the family to be buried there. On the same day, a special memorial service for friends and associates was held at Chelsea Old Church in London. The service was held amidst the chaos of the London Blitz: the following week, the church was badly damaged by German bombing.

Had he lived, Gresley would surely have been heart-broken to see the general operating conditions for trains during the Second World War: they were horrendous. Several regular former drivers described them as 'dangerous, difficult and at times prohibitive'.

All locomotives and rolling stock were blackened to prevent showing any light and most engines suffered from a crucial lack of regular maintenance. And Gresley's once-proud King's Cross top shed earned the tag of being called a 'disgrace': for long periods it was completely unable to service some of the country's finest locomotives.

But it wasn't all over yet for *Mallard* and her sisters. After the war, Sir Ronald Matthews, Sheffield's youngest ever Master Cutler, became the new chairman of the London & North Eastern Railway Company and started trying to restore the streamliners. A trial run in May 1946 boosted staff morale considerably but civil engineers, realising the potential damage and dangers to mainline tracks, suddenly imposed a 60mph speed restriction over the national rail networks.

On 29 September 1946, *Mallard* was renumbered No. 22. Just prior to the nationalisation of British Railways on 1 January 1948, she was sent home to Doncaster. She had recorded 54,209 miles since her last heavy repair and was repainted in her famous garter-blue livery. The newly formed Eastern Region selected *Mallard* as their own flagship – providing a welcome boost for both railway workers and the public. She was re-numbered as BR No. E22, and, after being briefly based at Grantham, from April that year she was allocated with a new corridor tender to King's Cross top shed, where she began to operate non-stop expresses to Scotland.

During the same year, *Mallard* took part in a series of locomotive exchanges. On several occasions she was reunited with her dynamometer car, which was used on a number of scheduled services, but she failed twice with mechanical problems, once in the Western Region, then again later, during a test run with the Southern Region. The exchanges provided an ideal opportunity for rail enthusiasts and train spotters, with a variety of mixed stock and locomotives appearing on cross-country services. The results established some important principles to be used in British Railways' forthcoming range of locomotives, but, sadly, streamlining was not one of them

With further cutbacks and lack of funding, however, the length of time and mileage between servicing increased for *Mallard* and other members of her illustrious class. During servicing from 27 May to 4 July 1952, she recorded 74,647 miles since her previous service and was repainted again, this time in British Railways green livery, a colour not unlike the famous racing green applied to sports cars. It could not have been more appropriate. By then, the A4s were the only class of streamlined locomotives in the country, the LMS's Princess Coronations having lost theirs to make maintenance easier. The rebuilt 'hush hush' locomotive No. 10000, now renumbered No. 60700, also retained streamlining, but she remained a one-off.

In May 1959, Mallard came close to losing her prestigious world record – it may have been pure accident, but it was Sir Nigel Gresley who was to blame. Not, of course, the venerable old gentleman himself, but his namesake, A4 class, No. 60007, *Sir Nigel Gresley*. On 23 May 1959, she gave an outstanding performance recording 112mph down Stoke Bank, hauling a Stephenson Locomotive Society Golden Jubilee tour. The engine might well have attempted a challenge to *Mallard*'s world record had not a vigilant inspector stepped forward and prevented driver Bill Hoole from going for glory.

By this time steam was being superseded by diesel and electric across Britain, and many important steam locomotives were scrapped. In the spring of 1960, however, *Mallard* got a reprieve: despite the onslaught of new diesel locomotives, she was hastily called back into mainline service. She made seven consecutive return trips from King's Cross to Newcastle, recording an amazing 3752 miles. *Mallard* worked several special excursions: on 12 June 1960, she ran from Alford in Lincolnshire to Edinburgh via the spectacular Settle to Carlisle route, and then ran a 'Northern

Rubber' special via the Calder Valley to Blackpool. She also worked the last northbound 'Elizabethan' in December 1961. On 20 December 1960, notification had been received that she would be preserved; nowadays it would be inconceivable that an engine as important as *Mallard* could be scrapped, but at the time ruthless efficiency generally took priority over conservation. Happily, her preservation order was finally confirmed on 29 August 1962.

She was eventually withdrawn from service on 25 April 1963, with a total mileage shown until December 1962 of 1,414,138 miles. She had proved herself a most remarkable locomotive.

After withdrawal, *Mallard* first returned to Doncaster works for mechanical attention, where she was restored to her original condition. In February 1963, she was taken to Nine Elms depot and later taken by road to the Clapham Railway Museum. Just before her unveiling at the museum, the man who had painted *Mallard* so beautifully in her colours before her record-breaking run in 1938, former Doncaster plant worker Herbert Betts, by then an old man in his seventies, was asked to help with the restoration. His son, Sidney, recalled: 'He was really chuffed when the management came down from the plant and asked if he was still fit enough to do it. But there was a slight problem when they brought the colour charts. My dad told them they were the wrong colours for the trains in York so they went and checked, and found out he was right. The problem was soon solved and he put on his overalls to meet up with his old pals for one last time.'

Despite her retirement, *Mallard*'s work on special excursion trains continued, and she remained a popular choice with the public. On 25 February 1964, she journeyed once again: from Doncaster to Nine Elms via Mexborough, Darnell, Staveley, Annesley, Nottingham Victoria and then via the Great Central line to Clapham Junction.

Technically, that should have been it for *Mallard*'s active career: the last steam trains ran for British Railways in 1968, and the nationalised firm immediately imposed a 'steam ban' for the privately owned locomotives around the country. They could potter up and down embryonic steam railways, but that was it. But in the 1970s the rules were relaxed and a limited number of locomotives were allowed back on the 'big railway'.

On 12 April 1975, *Mallard* ran from Stewart's Lane to York via Cricklewood and the Midland Main Line in preparation for the opening of the new National Railway Museum, where she remained. From 10 to 13 June 1977, *Mallard* was put on display at York for the railway station's centenary celebrations. And from 17 to 18 June 1978, she was displayed at Doncaster works for the 125th anniversary of the plant, though she wasn't in steam on this occasion.

In the 1980s, with the fiftieth anniversary of her record-breaking run in mind, engineers restored her to working order. On 25 March 1986, her travels resumed when she was employed on a unique run hauling a special train from York to Doncaster via Scarborough and Hull. *Mallard*'s exploits continued, and throughout that year she made a series of runs. On 10 June she ran from Doncaster to York via the Swinton and Knottingley line. On 9 July she travelled from York to Scarborough, returning via Hull and Selby, and on 31 August and 4 September she ran from York to Scarborough again, on the second occasion returning with a charter special in connection with an ASDA cricket festival. On 4 October she travelled from York to London Marylebone via Sheffield, Derby, Birmingham and Banbury. On 12 and 26 October, and again on 2 November, *Mallard* ran from London Marylebone to Stratford-upon-Avon and back again. She made her last journey that year on 8 November, when she travelled from London Marylebone to York, via Banbury, Birmingham, Derby and Sheffield.

In 1987 *Mallard* made another series of runs: on 25 and 26 April, from York to Harrogate and Leeds, and from York to

Scarborough return, for the Friends of National Railway Museum tenth anniversary charter train. On 16 May she journeyed from York to Carnforth and returned with an RSPB charter special: old lady she might be, but her owners were working her hard, and she performed superbly. In October she made her final runs for the year: on 2 October she ran from York to Doncaster with British Railways 2-10-0, No. 92220, *Evening Star*, the last steam locomotive built by British Railways. The following day she was one of the guests of honour at Doncaster works open day, before returning home to York with *Evening Star*.

In July 1988, as part of the fiftieth anniversary celebrations of her world record run, *Mallard* was once again in steam, and several family members of the original train crew travelled on this special excursion from Doncaster to Scarborough. Guests included Jean Delaney, the granddaughter of the driver, Joe Duddington, and her teenage son, Matthew. Another granddaughter of Duddington's, Pat Woodhead, remembered the run itself: 'Although I was too young to understand what had happened, I realised he had done something really exciting and was someone really special.'

Also included in the travelling party was Tom Bray, a retired slater and tiler, son of the fireman on the record run. He attended with his wife Betty and their son Cliff. Tom Bray commented: 'I was only seventeen then, and remember the record was attempted under a veil of secrecy. There was a lot of rivalry between the different regions in those days and news of the record wasn't released until the following day – when suddenly everyone connected with it became an instant celebrity. Today has been very enjoyable and a very emotional one. You have to feel proud about what my father and Joe Duddington achieved all those years ago.'

An enormous birthday cake commemorated *Mallard*'s unique achievement and numerous champagne corks popped in recognition. The cake was later given to Doncaster Royal Infirmary.

After lunch, the train and party continued to Scarborough, where hundreds more sun-drenched visitors again enjoyed the spectacle of *Mallard*'s arrival. By all accounts the reception was rapturous, a 'day for sunshine and strawberries'. Waxing lyrical, one journalist wrote: 'The grand old lady of steam, dressed in her best party finery, took centre stage once more to enjoy probably the most lavish steam train celebration Britain has ever seen. Fifty years to the day after setting the world's fastest time for a steam engine journey, *Mallard* returned to her home town of Doncaster to mark the achievement.'

Thousands packed every possible vantage point en route to see the beautiful old A4 in action again. Reports later claimed that onlookers crowded multi-storey car parks, station platforms, roadsides and river banks for 'what might be one last fleeting glimpse of a bygone age'. The journey was completed at a moderate 60mph, unlike the 126mph record achieved between Grantham and Peterborough half a century before, but still fast enough for this grand old lady. Her driver that day was Derek Richardson, one of six volunteers, who said: 'It was my luck that it was my turn for duty. This was the proudest day of my life.'

Stamp and postcard collectors also commemorated the anniversary. A combined effort from the Doncaster Postcard Club, the Doncaster Philatelic Society and the Rockware Philatelic Society, saw the launch of a special collector's item. This involved a joint postcard, with a full-colour scene of *Mallard,* together with a celebratory eighteen pence stamp and an individual Post Office anniversary cancellation. The franking service was organised by Peterborough Post Office, the nearest office to the scene of her triumph. It included an artist's impression of *Mallard* encircled by the fiftieth anniversary logo and the commemorative date of 3 July 1988.

Perhaps the magnitude of *Mallard*'s achievement can best be measured by press reports some fifty years after the record. A story in the *Daily Telegraph* by Ian Waller on 3 July 1988, headlined 'Steam Days to Remember', paid generous tribute to Gresley and his locomotive:

> The run was a triumph, the crowning achievement of Victorian technology and Gresley, the last of the great railway engineers and designers. He was a man of the twentieth century who studied aerodynamics and utilised the inventions of Bugatti to create *Mallard*'s gracefully curved wedge front, tapered wheel covers and funnel styled to lift the smoke clear of the cab.
>
> Every lover of steam has their favourite but for me Gresley's streamlined Pacifics are still the finest of the many beautiful locomotives produced during the years when steam reigned supreme. The extraordinary thing about steam engines is that the basic principles remain as Stephenson invented them, a boiler, steam cylinder or two with pistons and cranks and a sturdy lever to regulate the steam. There's nothing that a heavy hammer or spanner couldn't put right.

In the summer of 2003, *Mallard* made her most recent public appearance, outside the National Railway Museum, as part of the 150th-anniversary celebrations of Doncaster works on 26 and 27 July. The Doncaster 'plant', as it was known locally, had been the birthplace of more than 2500 locomotives and thousands of carriages and wagons, from the early Great Northern days onwards. The open weekend event was run in conjunction with the NRM, Wabtec Rail Limited and Doncaster Metropolitan Borough Council. It proved a very successful and emotional occasion, with a veterans' day on the Sunday when many former employees returned to revel in the nostalgia.

Many of Gresley's favourites returned for what might be a last curtain call. The clear crowd-pleasers were *Mallard* and *Flying Scotsman,* who performed alongside one of the oldest engines still in existence, Stirling No. 1 of 1870. The diesels were also represented by her spiritual successor of the 1960s, *Deltic,* No. D9000 *Royal Scots Grey*, and Doncaster-built 56 class No. 56031. The public were also treated to a rare glimpse of the 'Old Gentleman's Saloon' from the film *The Railway Children*, and some of the former luxury coaches that had worked with the 'Flying Scotsman' and 'Coronation' services. The event honoured a crucial period in Britain's railway heritage – and one that might never be repeated.

In the last few years has come the welcome news that three of *Mallard*'s sisters have not only been restored, but have all returned to working order. Operating on charter trains on the main line as well as running on heritage railways, they now give people who grew up with the legend the opportunity to experience an A4 in full cry. Sadly, the most famous of them all, the sublime *Mallard*, is permanently preserved at the National Railway Museum at York and seems unlikely ever to steam again. Kept magnificently, she stands next to the dynamometer car that proved so vital in recording her epic run.

Locomotive No. 60009, *Union of South Africa*, however, has been brilliantly restored to working order at the Severn Valley Railway in Shropshire, and is a regular performer on this line, also making appearances at the head of charter trains on the main line. Painted in her final livery of lined Brunswick green, and with the valances over the wheels removed, she represents an A4 at the peak of the 1950s. Since this book first appeared, locomotive No. 4464, *Bittern*, has undergone a lengthy restoration at the Mid Hants Watercress Line. Static for many years, she spent time disguised as *Silver Link*, but has returned to her original identity.

The final A4 in this country, No. 60007, no less than *Sir Nigel Gresley*, has also been restored, at the North Yorkshire Moors Railway in Grosmont. A regular performer on the main line for many years, she is also regularly worked on the demanding heritage railway where she is based, her huge power proving a tremendous asset.

The remaining two surviving A4s are both in North America, where they were presented to museums at the end of their service. Locomotive No. 4496, originally *Golden Shuttle*, was renamed *Dwight D Eisenhower* in September 1945, and on withdrawal in July 1963 (now renumbered 60008), was shipped to the American National Railway Museum, Green Bay, Chicago, where it is a somewhat unloved static exhibit. Locomotive No. 4489, *Dominion of Canada* (renumbered 60010), was also sent over the Atlantic after withdrawal, and resides today in the Montreal Railway Museum.

At the seventieth anniversary of *Mallard*'s run, her story still captures the imagination, and she remains by far the most popular exhibit at the National Railway Museum. And, pleasingly for Gresley, the concept he pioneered in this country of relatively short, high-speed trains continues to this very day around the world. It was the A4s which demonstrated the demand for high-speed travel, and though there were no steam successors, British Railways took the approach to heart with its streamlined diesel high-speed trains in the 1970s. The love and admiration in which *Mallard* is still held cannot be understated – the company which now runs long-distance trains from King's Cross to Edinburgh, the Great North Eastern Railway, has named its refurbished 225-class trains in her honour.

And the great engineer who began it all now has his own admirers, the Gresley Society, to honour his tremendous achievements. Recently, the Society (in conjunction with the Institution of Locomotive Engineers and a local parish council) erected a commemorative plaque in the Gresley family cemetery at Netherseale, South Derbyshire. On the top of the plaque is a small photograph of *Flying Scotsman* and a small ribbon-style inscription recording the dates of Sir Nigel Gresley's birth and death, 1876 and 1941.

But it is *Mallard*'s world record performance on a July day in 1938 that will remain Gresley's supreme achievement: at a time when the world faced economic and military ruin, *Mallard*'s performance challenged the might and power of the supposedly all-conquering Third Reich. She will be remembered forever for the record-breaking run which provided a vital national tonic at a critical time in world history.

At a time when railways were looking ahead at diesel traction, *Mallard* proved that conventional and cheap steam technology could match anything newer. During the war, she and her sisters proved able to haul loads of more than twenty coaches out of London, providing vital service. And after the war, these locomotives continued to give good service almost to the end of steam in the 1960s.

Mallard was, and remains, a design icon – a sculpture that symbolises everything good about rail travel in the 1930s. She's a symbol of luxury, of style, of intelligent design and brilliant construction. Even standing still, her design shouts out strength and speed, and even today, with the exception of the Eurostar services, there are no everyday passenger trains which travel faster than her record in Britain.

For Sir Nigel Gresley, Duddington, Bray and the uncounted drivers, firemen, fitters and cleaners who worked in the age of steam, *Mallard* stands testimony to their efforts and as a memorial to their brilliance. We will surely never see their like again.

Acknowledgements

should like to express thanks to my wife Kath, and my immediate family members, for enduring many missing hours spent researching, travelling or writing up notes – and for their continued support and encouragement. And I should like to mention, too, the help from the families of Joe Duddington and Tommy Bray.

In addition, I would like to praise the Gresley Society, and the following senior officials for their most generous advice during my extensive research for this book: Hon. Secretary Chris Nettleton; vice-presidents Dr Geoffrey Hughes, Michael Joyce and Peter N. Townend. And especially Dr Hughes for his willingness to share valuable information concerning Sir Nigel Gresley's early years, and his extensive knowledge of the gradual development of *Mallard*.

I should also like to express my appreciation to the editor of *The Gresley Observer*, Dr Peter Rodgers, to registrar of archives Sue McNaughton, and to the Gresley Society chairman, committee members and general members for allowing the use of back copies and memories contained within their magazine; and providing some fascinating archive material. Thanks too, to former engine driver Norman Taylor for his generous assistance and encouragement, and to a host of other individuals for sharing their nostalgic memories.

Also great credit to the following additional organisations:
The National Railway Museum, York
The archive department at the National Railway Museum
The Friends of the National Railway Museum, York
The National Newspaper Records archive in London

The *Stamford and Rutland Mercury*
The *Doncaster Free Press*
The *Yorkshire Post*
Yorkshire Television
The editor, *The Times*, London
Railway Magazine
The editor, the *Daily Express*
The Lancashire & Yorkshire Railway History Society
North Wales Newspapers Ltd.

A special mention must be made of Graham Coster and Phoebe Clapham at Aurum Press, my agent John Pawsey, and book editor Andrew Roden, without whose time, effort and support this book would never have happened.

And my sincere apologies to anyone else who may have helped with the production but whom I have omitted in error. Every contribution, no matter how large or small, was fully appreciated.

Bibliography

Special thanks to Dr Geoffrey Hughes for many helpful discussions and for allowing me access to his extensive research, both notes and personal photographs. Praise too should go to the officials at the National Railway Museum, to whom I am very grateful for permission to use extracts from documents at their railway archive and library.

Anyone interested in knowing more about the advance of the LNER, Mallard and/or Sir Nigel Gresley's distinguished career should consult the following important books of reference, to which I am indebted:

Brown, Francis, *Nigel Gresley: Locomotive Engineer*, Ian Allan Publishing, 1961

Cook, A.F. (ed), *ABC British Ralways Locomotives: Combined Volume 1951*, Ian Allan Publishing, 1951

Day Lewis, Sean, *Bulleid: Last Giant of Steam*, George Allen & Unwin, 1968

Hasted, Derrick, 'Sir Nigel Gresley: The Personality Behind the Engineer', in *40 Years On*, booklet published to mark the special train hauled by *Sir Nigel Gresley* on 23 May 1999

Hughes, Geoffrey, *Sir Nigel Gresley: The Engineer and his Family*, The Oakwood Press, 2001

Middleton, Allan, *It's Quicker by Rail: The History of LNER Advertising*, Tempus Publishing Ltd, 2002

Morrison, Gavin, *Glory Days, Gresley A4s: The LNER's Streamlined Pacific Locomotives*, Ian Allan Publishing, 2001

Murray, A.J., *Streamlined Steam: Britain's 1930s Luxury Expresses*, David & Charles, 1994

Simmons, Jack & Biddle, Gordon (eds), *The Oxford Companion to British Railway History*, Oxford University Press, 1997

The Story of the Train, National Railway Museum, 2001

Whitehouse, Patrick & Thomas, David St John, *LNER 150: The London &
North Eastern Railway: A Century and a Half of Progress*, David &
Charles, 2002

Index

A1 Pacific class 39–41, 42, 78
A3 Pacific class 42, 78, 89, 124, 150
A4 Pacific class x, 89, 90–92, 105, 106, 108, 109, 110, 115, 116, 117, 119, 120, 122–5, 127, 128, 130, 131, 150, 153, 155, 164–5
Aachen Technical College 100
Aberdeen 5, 6, 7, 48, 84, 108, 109
Adkinson, Bernard 133, 137, 139, 142
Adler (*Eagle*) 59
aerodynamic drag 93
aeroplanes 24, 45, 65
airscrew propeller 59, 60
airships 24, 94, 116
Alford, Lincolnshire 158
Allen, Cecil J. 83, 95, 96, 104, 105, 113, 115, 120–21, 152
Allerton, Lord 16
Alne, near York 49
Alsace 62
Altoona testing plant 56
American National Railway Museum, Green Bay, Chicago 164
Annesley 159
Arbroath 111
Archangel Northern Railway, Russia 43
Ardsley 97
Aspinall, John 14
Association for the Advancement of the Sciences 60
Association of British Locomotive Engineers 100
Atlantic No. 3290 148
Atlantics (4-4-2 designs) 21, 40, 50, 107, 130, 146, 147
Auden, W.H. 81
Austria 118, 150
Autobahn 68

Banbury 160
Banff, Canada 51
Bannister, Eric 125–6, 137, 140, 141, 147

Bantam Cock 156
Barcelona 150
Barham House, St Leonard's, Sussex 12
Barkston South Junction, Lincolnshire 109, 115, 132, 137, 141, 142
Barton-under-Needwood, Derbyshire 12
BBC 147, 148
Beattock 7
Bell, Robert 25–6
Bentley, W.O. 62
Beresford, A.E. 30, 123
Berlin 69, 103
Berlin to Hamburg line 59, 65, 70, 71, 73, 74, 101, 102, 105, 153
Berlin-Charlottenberg Technical College 100
Berlin-Grunewald locomotive test centre 100
Betts, Herbert 159
Betts, Sidney 159
Bing 45
Birmingham 3, 160
Bittern (No. 4464) 164
Black 5 locomotive 78
Blackpool 159
Blackshirts 88
Blairgowrie (steamship) 122
blastpipe 124–5
Bohemia 118
Borsig factory, Berlin 101
Bournemouth 16
Brackenbury, A.G. 138
Brademann, Richard 68
Bradford 109, 116
Branson, Sir Richard 46
Bray, Betty 161
Bray, Cliff 161
Bray, Tommy 131, 138, 140, 147, 149, 150, 161, 166
brick arch (in firebox) 106
Bridge of Allan, Scotland 32
British Empire 110
British Empire Exhibition (1924) 39

British Railways 113, 158, 160, 161
Britten, Benjamin 81
Brown, Charles 96
Brownshirts 68, 73
Bugatti, Carlo 62
Bugatti, Ettore 62–7, 69, 72, 84, 86, 90, 92, 93, 108, 115, 125
Bugatti railcars 64–5, 67, 72–3
Bugatti Royal 63, 64
Bulleid, Oliver 69, 125
  background and earlier career 28
  appointed Gresley's principal technical assistant 28–9
  war service 29, 43
  returns to Gresley's circle 29
  as the ideas man 29
  relationship with Gresley 34, 35
  and Dorpmoller 61
  and Bugatti 63, 64
  tries to find out about the *Flying Hamburger* 73–4
  and the London–Leeds record 83
  and *Cock o' the North*'s French trials 85–7
  friendship with Wagner 100
  attends German trials 104
  at *Sir Nigel Gresley* ceremony 122
  becomes CME of the Southern Railway 123
  launch of *Merchant Navy* Pacific 156
Burfoot (driver) 115
Burley, Leslie 120, 148
Burton on Trent 11
Bury, Oliver 29

Caerphilly Castle (No. 4073) 39
Calder Valley 159
Caledonian Railway 2, 6, 7, 32
Canadian Pacific Railway 51
  2-10-4 locomotive 51
Carling, Denis 133, 139, 141, 142–4, 146, 152–3
Carlisle 2, 3, 7, 114
Carnforth 161
Cassidy, Sir Maurice 51, 128
Castle class 39, 41, 76
Centenary (No. 2555) 42
Chamberlain, Neville 155
Channel Tunnel project 57
Chapelon, André 52, 69, 105, 125
  birth and background 52
  CME, Paris–Orleans Railway 52–3

start of association with Gresley 52
personality 53
innovative ideas 53–4
American design factors 54
4-6-2 and 4-8-0 designs 54–5
and compound test engine No. 10000 55–6
French national test centre 56, 85
and *Cock o' the North* 85, 86, 87
reports activity on the German steam front 90
criticism of 93
Kylchap exhaust system 144
Chelsea Old Church, London 156
chime whistles, removal during Second World War 155–6
Church Gresley, Derbyshire 12
Churchill, Randolph 95, 96
Churchill, Sir Winston 57, 69, 95
City and Guilds Engineering College, London 66
City class locomotives 9
City of Truro (No. 3440) 9, 83
Clapham Junction 159
Clapham Railway Museum 159
Clarke, Tom 113, 114
coaches 24, 45, 71
Cock o' the North P2 class (No. 2001) 84–8
  Gresley's guinea pig 84
  the most powerful express locomotive in Britain 84
  driving wheels 84
  wedge-shaped front 84–5
  long and rigid wheelbase 85
  high maintenance 85
  French tests 85–7
  shown at a prestigious French railway exhibition 87
Collett, Charles 39, 41, 76
Cologne 69
Cologne–Berlin service 72
Cologne–Hamburg service 72
Colwyn Bay 113
Comet 79
competition
  London to Scotland races 2–8
  running times 4–7
  parallel running 6
  plans to abolish 24
  from other forms of passenger transport 24, 44–5, 65

LNER/GWR trials (1925) 39 41
German diesel-electric tests start another
    race 59–60
Coronation Scot competes with Gresley's
    royal tributes 112
compound test engine No. 10000 55–6, 57
compounding 54
Cooper, Austin 32
Coronation (No. 6220) 113, 115–16, 136,
    138, 139, 142, 148
'Coronation' service 45, 108, 110, 115–16,
    118–19, 120, 131, 132, 133, 164
'Coronation Scot' service 112–14
corridor tender 49–50, 55
Coventry 79
Crewe, Cheshire 3, 7, 11, 13, 76, 111–14,
    121
Cricklewood 160
Cross Gates, near Leeds 57

Daily Express 149
Daily Mail 95
Daily Telegraph 163
Dalby, Professor W.E. 66, 126, 137
Dandridge, Cecil 120
    war service 43
    press and publicity chief 43
    asks Gill to produce a unique new
        typeface 43–4
    marketing ideas 45
    and the press 46
    series of promotional challenges 46
    commissions seaside town posters 80
    best-kept station competitions and garden
        displays 81
    and *Mallard* 134
Darlington 2, 42, 55, 56, 106, 133, 134
    Mechanical Engineer Design Testing and
        Performance Section 151–2
Darnell 159
Davey Paxman, Colchester 52
Day, Frank 129
Dean, William 76
Deauville 65, 67
Deginthin 59
Delaney, Jean 161
Delaney, Matthew 161
Derby 11, 76, 160
Deutsche Reichsbahn (DR) 59, 60, 65, 67,
    68, 69, 70, 71, 72, 89, 99, 103, 104,
    116, 117, 118, 146

diesel power
    French trials on high-speed diesel electric
        sets 58
    German testing of streamlined high-speed
        diesel railcars 59
    German light-weight diesel sets 99
    diesels represented at National Railway
        Museum event (2003) 163
Doble steamcar 103
Dobson, Percy 134, 139, 142, 145
Dolphingstone, near Prestonpans 82
Dominion of Canada (No. 4489 renumbered
    60010) 110, 115, 164
Doncaster 2, 40, 107, 149, 159–62
Doncaster works 14, 19, 30, 33, 35–8, 41,
    49, 56, 62, 90, 91, 94, 106, 118, 127,
    129, 130, 133, 137, 142, 155, 160, 163
Dorpmoller, Dr Julius 60–61, 68, 70, 104
Dortmund engine office No. 2 100
Douglas, Reverend William 11
Drakelow, South Derbyshire 12
Dreyfuss, Henry 93
driving wheels 84
Duchess of Hamilton 164
Duddington, Joe 130–1, 138, 139, 143, 144,
    145, 147, 149–50, 153–4, 161, 166
Duddington, Marjorie 149
Dwight D Eisenhower (originally *Golden
    Shuttle*) 164
dynamometer cars 83, 85, 86, 88, 103, 109,
    131–2, 137, 139–42, 144–7, 157, 164

Earl Marischal P2 engine 85
East Coast Main Line 41, 75, 82, 129
East Coast service 73, 74, 96
    route to Scotland 2–7, 9
    German test proposals 81–2
Edge, Douglass 133, 136, 139, 141–2, 145
Edinburgh 2, 6, 7, 47, 49, 55, 57, 84, 109,
    115, 158, 165
Edward VIII, King (later Duke of Windsor)
    108, 117, 149
Einhert's steam locomotives 100
Einhets development programme 60
Eisenbahn-Zentralamt, Berlin 100
Essendine 144, 145
Essendine bank 88
Euston, London 2, 6, 77, 79, 112, 113, 114,
    120
Evening Star (No. 92220) 161
Everton 140

Felstead (No. 2743) 42
56 class No. 56031 163
First World War 19, 23, 26, 29, 30, 76
Fliegende Hamburger train (*Flying Hamburger*)
    60–1, 67–75, 81, 83, 101, 105, 156
Flying Fox 40
Flying Scotsman A1 Pacific (No. 4472) 45, 55,
    69, 90, 108, 165
    first appears (1923) 39
    cost 39
    at the British Empire Exhibition (1924) 39
    restaurant cars 48
    popularity of 47, 50, 93
    non-stop King's Cross–Newcastle run 46,
        48–9
    non-stop London–Edinburgh run (world
        non-stop steam record) 49, 50, 107
    luxury features 48
    and compound test engine No. 10000 55
    reduced journey times on London–Edin-
        burgh route 57–8
    London–Leeds trial achieves new record
        (1934) 82–3
    at the National Railway Museum 163, 164
'Flying Scotsman' service 45, 47–9, 50,
    57–8, 90, 108, 164
Forth Bridge 5
four-cylinder locomotives 20, 21
Fowler, Sir Henry 77
France
    and diesel power 58
    new test facility (1933) 58
    track speed safety regulations 72
Franco-Prussian war 4
Frankfurt Main 69
freight trains
    importance of 17, 119
    shortage of 17
    0-6-0 chassis 18
    Robinson's design 26
Friesack station 104
Furth 59

Gallitzin, Princess Olga 43
Gamages stores, London 45
Garbe, Robert 100
Gard du Nord, Paris 87
Gateshead shed 50, 106, 109
Gay Crusader (No. 4477) 107
George V, King 90, 106
George VI, King 108

German 05 class 99, 101–4, 153
    No. 001 101–2
    No. 002 99, 101–5
    No. 003 102
German Railways *see* Deutsche Reichsbahn
Germany
    aims to acquire an Empire like Britain's
        4–5
    trials 59, 102–5, 120
    diesel-electric developments 59–61
    Hitler pumps funds into the railway sys-
        tem 68
    promotion of the *Flying Hamburger* 68–9
    test proposals 81–2, 83
    Night of the Long Knives (1934) 88
    Papyrus defeats the German railcar propos-
        al 89
    world speed record (1935) 103, 112, 114
    Hindenburg disaster 116
    Night of the Broken Glass (1938) 118
    occupation of Austria 118
    Mallard breaks German record 1, 144–5,
        146, 153
Gestapo 73
Gill, Eric 43–4
'Gill Sans' typeface 44
Glasgow 2, 48, 114
Glasgow, Ben 40, 95
GNR *see* Great Northern Railway
Godfrey, Geoffrey 52, 77
Godfrey, Violet (née Gresley) 51, 52, 77,
    156
Goebbels, Joseph 68–9, 72, 104, 117
Goering, Herman 104
Golden Fleece 109
Golden Shuttle (No. 4496) (renamed *Dwight
    D Eisenhower*) 109, 165
Gorton works 30, 36
Grantham, Lincolnshire ix, 1, 7, 83, 89,
    137, 138, 140, 142, 143, 147, 155, 157,
    162
Great Central line 159
Great Central Railway 23, 25, 26
Great Eastern Railway 25, 66
Great North Eastern Railway 165
Great North of Scotland Railway 25
Great Northern (No. 1470) 28
    and the K4 class Pacific 22
    first appearance in public (April 1922) 22
Great Northern Railway (GNR) 97, 129,
    130, 163

Gresley's chassis designs 14
the board's attitude to Gresley 15, 16
shortage of freight trains 17
and the 2-7-0 with three cylinders 19
and the K4 class Pacific 22
the new LNER operation 25
Bulleid works for 28
carriages 131
Great Western Pacific 22
Great Western Railway (GWR) 76
formation of 25
competitions 2, 9
2-6-0 chassis (mogul) 18
four-cylinder locomotives 20
LNER/GWR trials (1925) 39–41
LNER takes the world non-stop steam
record from 50
Stanier at 76, 77, 78
Swindon test plant 56
Green Man pub, Little Bytham (later
Mallard) 151
Gresley, Ethel (née Fullager) 14, 51
Gresley, Sir Herbert Nigel
birth (1876) 11
background and childhood 11–12
education 12–13
apprenticed to the LNWR, Crewe 11, 13
rapid promotions 14–15
personality 15, 27, 33–4
horrific injury 16
appointed CME, GNR 16, 38
uses old designs at first 17
designs K1, a 2-7-0 type and K2 19
war service 19
designs a 2-7-0 with three cylinders
19-20
location of the valve gear 20–21
K3 introduced 21
experiment with Ivatt engine No. 3279 21
inspired by K4 class Pacific 22
constructs the Great Northern 22
appointed CME, LNER 26–7
his responsibilities 27
and marketing of the LNER 31
relationship with Bulleid 34
as a 'hands-on' CME 33–8
his third Pacific (Flying Scotsman) 39, 48
LNER/GWR trials 39, 40
produces A3s 42
corridor tenders 49–50
and death of his wife 51

love of wildfowl, especially the mallard
51–2, 123
start of association with Chapelon 52
'hush-hush' compound locomotive No.
10000 55–6, 57
static locomotive testing plant proposal
56–7
headphones idea 58
told to cut back on steam loco
development 58
and Dorpmoller 61
and Bugatti 62–7
experiments with streamlining steam
locomotives 65–7
and Germany's redevelopment
programme 69
travels on the Flying Hamburger 74–5
relationship with Stanier 77
firm belief that steam could rule the day
84, 121
and Cock o' the North 84, 85, 87–8
new A4s 91–2
overseas criticism of his locomotives 93
friendship with Wagner 100
and Silver Fox's 1936 record 107–8
failed attempt to get record back from
LMS (1937) 114–15
financial constraints 119–20
honours 121, 122
safety matters 124
smoke issue 125–7
decision to challenge speed record again
127–30
preparations for the attempt 133–5
unable to attend the record attempt 136
told of Mallard's success 146
unveiling of his final steam engine and first
electric engine 156
death, burial and memorial service (1941)
156
tribute to 163
Gresley, Joanna (née Wilson) 11, 12, 16,
156
Gresley, Reverend Norman 11
Gresley, Roger 156
Gresley, Violet see Godfrey, Violet
Gresley Society 87, 165
Gutteridge (driver) 89
GWR see Great Western Railway

Hamburg 103

Harrison, Freddie 40
Harrison, J.H. 21, 35–6
Harrogate 160
Harwich 81, 86
Hassall, John 32
Hatfield 140
Henschel V8 locomotive (No. 19.001)
    117–18
Henschel-Wegman-Zug 103
Henschen & Sons 117
Heusinger-Waldegg, Admiral 102–3
Heydrich, Reinhard 104
Highland Railway 25
Himmler, Heinrich 104
Hindenburg, Paul von 67
Hindenburg airship 116
Hitchin, Hertfordshire 96, 140
Hitler, Adolf 67–8, 69, 103, 104, 116, 117,
    118, 155
Hoather, Max 134–5, 138
Hoene (German driver) 103
Holcroft, Harold 100, 104
Holme 137, 140
Hoole, Bill 158
Hornby 45–6
Horwich, Lancashire 13, 76
Hull 160
Hull & Barnsley Railway 25
Humorist (No. 2751) 124
Huntingdon 140

Imperial Airways 46
Institute of Transport 82
Institution of Locomotive Engineers 66,
    100, 101, 104, 121, 165
International Railway Congress 30
Ivatt, Henry 15, 16, 21, 28, 38, 62
Ivatt Atlantics 21, 130, 146
Ivatt engine No. 3279 21

Jackson, James 52
Jagow, von (German railwayman) 103
Jarrow Hunger March (1936) 110–11
Jarvis, Christopher 134, 139, 142
Jenkins, Inspector Sam 133, 134, 138, 140,
    141
Johansen, F.C. 66, 67
Joyce, Michael 121
Jubilee class locomotives 78

K1 locomotive 19

K2 locomotive 19
K3 locomotive 21, 22
K4 class Pacific 22
Karstadt 59
Keighley 160
'Kesselsieve' system of stored superheat 102
King class 76
King's Cross, London 2, 5, 6, 31, 35, 36,
    37, 40, 43, 47, 49, 50, 55, 61, 64, 75,
    77, 81, 88, 95, 97, 106, 107, 109, 115,
    116, 120, 123, 129, 130, 131, 133, 136,
    138, 146, 147, 149, 151, 153, 157, 158,
    165
Kinnaber Junction, near Montrose 6
Kircaldy 109
Kruckenburg, Dr F. 60, 70
Kylchap double chimney 124
Kylchap exhaust system 54, 55–6, 144

Lakehurst, New Jersey 11
Lancashire & Yorkshire Railway 13
Langford Bridge 137, 140
Langhams (German driver) 103
Le Clair, Mr (of Westinghouse team) 138,
    142
Le Havre 67
Leeds 80, 109, 116, 130, 160
Lewis, John 113
Little Bytham 83, 144, 150–51
Liverpool 79
Liverpool Street, London 36
Llandudno Junction 113
LMS *see* London Midland and Scottish Rail-
    way
LNER *see* London and North Eastern Rail-
    way
LNWR *see* London & North Western Rail-
    way
Loewy, Raymond 93
London and North Eastern Railway (LNER)
    132
    formation of 25
    Whitelaw appointed first chairman 25
    Wedgwood appointed chief general man-
        ager 25–6
    Gresley appointed chief mechanical engi-
        neer 26–7
    financial problems 31, 36, 92, 119
    marketing 31–3, 43–7, 80, 90
    LNER/GWR trials (1925) 39–41
    punctuality 44, 106–7

rivalry with London Midland 49, 76, 84,
  89, 108
corridor tenders 49–50
and Channel Tunnel plan 57
wind-resistance methods 67
and the *Flying Hamburger* 74
and secondary lines 80
slogans 80
successful 'Silver Jubilee' service 107
government funding 107
and the Jarrow Hunger March 110–11
key staff members 120
carriages 131
Matthews becomes chairman 157
London & North Western Railway Company
  (LNWR) 2, 3, 7, 11
London & South Western Railway, competitions 9
London Midland and Scottish Railway
  (LMS) 124
  formation of 25
  ashtrays 47
  rivalry with LNER 49, 76, 84, 89, 108
  and wind-resistance methods 67
  inherits locomotive works 76
  reorganisation 76
  Stanier becomes CME 77
  massive commercial interests in Europe
    77
  restructuring 77
  modernisation plant 78
  speed trials 78–9
  and secondary lines 79–80
  marketing 80
  new high-speed British record (1937)
    113–14, 121
  Mallard breaks the record 144, 146, 152
London–Aberdeen 108–9
London–Newcastle service 89, 90
Love, Mr (senior messenger) 129
Luftwaffe 156
Luty, J. 95

Mallard (No. 4468)
  choice of name 123
  of special significance to Gresley 123–4
  total building cost 124
  blastpipe 124–5
  streamlining 125, 136
  smoke dispersion 127
  world-record-breaking run (1938) 1,

    136–48, 165–6
  overheated big end 145, 146, 152–3
  headline news around the world 148, 150
  debate about the record 151–3
  repainted in jet blackout livery 155
  renumbered and repainted blue 157
  flagship of the Eastern Region 157
  special excursions 158–9
  preservation order 159
  withdrawn from service (1963) 159
  subsequent runs 159–63
  fiftieth anniversary of her world record
    run (1988) 161–3
  at the National Railway Museum 163, 164
Mallard pub, Little Bytham 151
Manchester 3, 7
Manchester University 121
Märklin 45
Marlborough College 12
Marylebone Station, London 122, 160
Mason, Frank 81
Master Royale 63
Matthews, Sir Ronald 157
Maybach, Dr Karl 59, 60, 70, 73, 74, 75,
  81, 101
Maybach Motor Works engines 70
Menzies, John 58
Merchant Navy Pacific 156
Mexborough 159
Michelin 64
Mid Hants Watercress Line 164
Midland Main Line 160
Midland Railway 23
  sets up its own service to Scotland 3–4
  admits third class passengers to all of its
    services 4
  upgrades third class, scrapping second
    class 4
Mikado-class engines 54, 99
mileage posts 8
Minden 117
miners' strike (1893–4) 13
model railways 45–6, 104
moguls (2-6-0 arrangement) 18, 19
Montreal Railway Museum 164
Montrose 111
Moravia 118
Mosley, Oswald 88
motor vehicles 24, 45, 65
Munich 69, 73
Mussolini, Benito 103

National Physical Laboratory (NPL), Teddington 66, 67, 125, 126
National Railway Museum, York 47, 132, 147, 160, 163, 165
nationalisation 1, 23, 59, 155
Nauen 102
Nazi Party 61, 104
NER *see* North Eastern Railway
Netherseale, near Swadlincote, Derbyshire 11, 12, 51, 156, 165
Neustadt Dosse 104
Neve, Eric 120
New Barnet 148
New York Central line 54, 99
Newbould, Frank 32
   Britain's Fastest Streamlined Train 81
Newcastle 2, 7, 26, 49, 56, 75, 81, 89, 90, 105, 106, 109, 115, 118, 120, 158
Newsome, Norman 129–33, 136–9, 141
Newton Heath, near Manchester 14
Nicholson, Leslie 139–40
Night Mail (publicity film) 81
Nine Elms depot 159
Nock, O.S. 113
Nord Pacific locomotive 87
Nordmann, Dr 104
North Berwick 128
North British Railway 3, 25
North Eastern Railway (NER) 2, 25, 26, 30, 132
'Northern Rubber' special 158–9
Nottingham Victoria 159
Nuremberg 59, 69

observation saloons 115–16
ocean liners 24, 45
Offord curves 97
Olley, Captain Gordon 46
Olympic Games (1936) 116
Orleans 86
Ouse River 47

P2 class 84, 85–6, 87
Pacifics (4-6-2 designs) 21, 38, 48, 50, 70, 78–82, 84, 92–3, 94, 108, 110, 125, 131
Paddington, London 40, 150
Palace of Engineering, British Empire Exhibition 39
Papyrus A3 class (No. 2750) 83, 89, 90, 93
Paris 65, 67, 87

Paris–Le Havre line 72
Paris–Orleans Railway 53
Paulinenaue 102, 103
Pendennis Castle 40, 41
Pennsylvania Railroad Company 22, 56
Peppercorn, A.H. 122
Persimmon (No. 2549) 47
Perth 7, 48
Peterborough 1, 2, 83, 88, 133, 137, 140, 142, 145, 146, 147, 162
Pibworth, Albert 40, 50
piston valves 42
Plymouth 9, 40
Poland, invasion of 155
Post Office 81, 162
posters 32, 44, 45, 80–81
Potters Bar 139, 140
premium apprentice scheme 35–6, 37
Preston 2, 8
Preston, Leslie Parker 30–31
Princess Coronation class 78, 158
Princess Coronation (No. 6229) 164
Princess Elizabeth LMS Pacific (No. 6201) 78
Princess Royal LMS Pacific (No. 6200) 78, 79, 112
Prussian Railways 100
pupillage 35–6
Purvis, Tom 32–3

QSA vacuum brake system 132, 135
Queen Elizabeth (ocean liner) 81
Queen Mary (ocean liner) 81
Queen's course, Gleneagles 128
Quicksilver (no. 2510) 92, 95, 106, 107

Railway Centenary Exhibition (Darlington, 1925) 42–3
Railway Gazette 51
Railway Magazine 120
Railways Act (1921) 24
Rainhill Trials (1729) 2
Raven, Sir Vincent 26, 30
re-privatisation 1
recession 92
Remnant, P.T.W. 138, 142, 143
Renault 64
Richardson, Derek 162
Riddles, R.A. 113–14
Robinson, John 26
Robson, Tom 133
Rocket 2

rolling stock 9, 24, 27–8, 48, 53, 54, 65, 74, 93, 101, 104, 107, 132
Roosen, Richard 117
Roth (German railwayman) 103
Royal Albert Hall, London 63
Royal Border Bridge, Berwick 46, 47
Royal Scot class 79
Royal Scots Grey Deltic (No. D9000) 163
RSPB charter special 161
Rugby 2, 57
Runciman, Sir Walter 121–2

S-Bahn services 116
Salisbury Hall, near St Albans 51, 52, 123
Sandy, Bedfordshire 97, 140
São Paulo railway, Brazil 29
Scarborough 160, 161, 162
Schienenzeppelin 60, 70
Scotland, races to 2–8
'Scotsman' service 4, 5, 8
Scottish railways 23
Second World War 155–7
Selby 5, 160
Settle–Carlisle Railway 3
Settle–Carlisle route 158
Severn Vallery Railway, Shropshire 164
Shap Summit, Lake District 7
Sheffield 3, 157, 160
Silver Fox (no. 2512) 92, 95, 106, 108, 128, 143, 144
'Silver Jubilee' service 90, 91, 105–10, 115, 118, 120
Silver King (no. 2511) 92, 95, 106, 109
Silver Link (no. 2509) 92, 94, 105–6, 107, 110, 164
  trial a huge success (1935) 95–8
Simpson, Mrs *see* Duchess of Windsor
Sir Nigel Gresley 122, 158, 164
Sir Ralph Wedgwood (No. 4469) 156
Skegness, Lincolnshire 32
smoke
  constantly obscures a driver's view 65–6
  horizontal wedge lifts smoke over the top of the loco 66
  problem solved 125–7
Society of Locomotive Engineers 57
Southern Railway (SR) 25, 67, 123
Southern region 157
Spanish Civil War 150
Sparshatt, Bill 82, 89, 95, 107, 120
speed
  of Stephenson's *Rocket* 2
  London to Aberdeen world record time (1895) 6–7
  Britain's early steam records 9–10
  buzz-word of the period 3
  London-Scotland speed trials 2–8
  Plymouth–London run (1904) 9
  Flying Scotsman's world non-stop steam record 49, 50
  German trials 59, 102–5
  Bugatti railcars 65
  Flying Hamburger 60, 70
  Princess Elizabeth (London–Glasgow) 78
  Stanier's trials for LMS 79
  Flying Scotsman London–Leeds trial achieves new record (1934) 82–3
  Papyrus's new world speed record (1935) 89, 90
  German world speed record (1935) 103, 112, 114
  Silver Fox's 1936 record 108
  LMS high-speed British record (1937) 113–14, 121
  Mallard's world record 1, 136–48, 165–6
speedometers 8
Speer, Albert 68
Spencer, Bert 30, 41–2, 122, 141
SR *see* Southern Railway
Stafford 2
Stamford Mercury 150
Stamp, Sir Josiah 76–7
Stanier, Joan 77
Stanier, William 108
  education and early career 76
  war service 76
  CME at LMS 77
  relationship with Gresley 77
  investigates failures in service 77–8
  interested in the potential for steam-turbine motive power 78
  modernisation plant 78
  locomotive creation 78
  brake trials 79
  and secondary lines 79–80
  lack of construction at major terminals 80
  and Wagner 100
  attends German trials 104, 105
  launches new high-speed service 112
  and high-speed British record 114

congratulates Gresley on *Mallard*'s record
148
starting tractive effort 39
static locomotive testing plant proposal
56–7
Staveley 159
steam locomotive
  invention of (1804) 1–2
  reputation for being dirty, noisy and
    smelly 99
Stettiner Bahnhof 116
Stephenson, George 43
Stephenson, Robert 2, 53, 59, 102, 163
Stevenage 97, 137
Stewart's Lane 160
Stirling No. 1 163
Stirling, Patrick 130
Stoke Bank 89, 162
Stoke summit 85, 88, 115, 143, 147
Stoke Tunnel 83, 143
Stratford Works 31, 66
streamlining
  Wagner tests his theories 100–101
  post-war 158
stroboscopic cameras 54
Stubley, Richard 140
Stuttgart 69
Sudetenland 118
superheat 99, 102
Swindon test plant 56
Swindon works 76, 77
Swinton 160
Symes, Barney 36–8, 87–8, 118–19

Tay Bridge 5
Taylor, A. 95, 96, 97–8
Taylor, G.H. 140
Teasdale, William 31–3, 43, 120
Third Reich 68, 74, 101, 102, 105, 150,
  153, 166
Thompson, Edward 30, 122
three-cylinder locomotives 19–22, 84,
  100–101
through ticketing 23
Toplis, Tommy 95
Tours 86
Tours Grand Prix 63
Townend, P.N. 96
Trevithick, Richard 1–2
Trouville–Deauville 73
Turnditch, Derbyshire 16

two-cylinder locomotives 20, 21
Union of South Africa (No. 60009) 110, 164
Unter den Linden 116
Usworth (steamship) 122
V1 three-cylinder tank engine 37
valve gear 20–21, 41–2, 52, 84
Versailles Treaty (1919) 118
vertical wedge design, flawed 93
Viscount Churchill 41
Vitry-sur-Seine test facility, near Paris 58,
  87

Wabtec Rail Limited 163
Waddington, John, of Leeds 45
wages 13, 36
Wagner, Dr Richard 59, 60, 67, 68, 99
  early career 100
  English connections 100, 105
  wants to exploit his streamlining theories
    100–101
  'High Speed and the Steam Locomotive'
    lecture 101
  attends German trials 104
  Witte replaces 118
Wall Street crash (1929) 51, 52, 62, 63, 64
Waller, Ian 163
Watford 114
Watton-on-Stone 52, 146, 156
Webster (at the GNR) 28
Wedgwood, Sir Ralph Lewis 25–8, 31, 32,
  43, 69, 75, 76, 82, 93, 95–6, 120, 122,
  127
Welwyn Garden City 137, 140
West Coast service route to Scotland 2,
  4–7, 9
'West Riding Ltd' service 109, 110, 116,
  118
Western region 157
Westinghouse, Freinville works, near Paris
  28
Westinghouse QSA brake valves 124
Westinghouse Brake Company 132, 133,
  137, 142
WH Smith 58
Whitelaw, William 25, 26, 81, 82, 90, 96,
  120, 128
Whitmore Bank 113
wind resistance 66, 67, 92, 127
wind-tunnel testing 66, 67, 70, 125
Windsor Castle 41
Windsor, Duchess of 117

Windsor, Edward, Duke of *see* Edward VIII, King

Wintour, Francis 28, 122

Witte, Friedrich 99, 117, 118

Wittenberg 100, 103, 104, 105

Wolff, Adolf 99, 101

Wood Green waterworks, London 132, 136, 137, 140

Woodhead, Pat 161

Woolwich Arsenal 30

Workers' Movement 88

Wright Brothers 125

Wycliffe College, Gloucestershire 76

York 2, 5, 7, 26, 48, 55, 107, 130, 149, 156, 160, 161

York, Duke and Duchess of (later George VI and Queen Elizabeth) 42–3

Zeebrugge 86

'Zeppelin' wind tunnels 70

Zeppelin works, Germany 125